Loving
Someone
Else's
Child

Loving Someone Else's Child

Angela
Elwell Hunt

 Tyndale House Publishers, Inc.
Wheaton, Illinois

Cover photograph © 1991 by Jim Whitmer

Scripture quotations are from the *Holy Bible,* New International Version. Copyright © 1973, 1978, 1984 International Bible Society. Used
by permission of Zondervan Bible Publishers.

Library of Congress Cataloging-in-Publication Data

Hunt, Angela Elwell, date
  Loving someone else's child / by Angela Elwell Hunt.
      p.   cm.
  Includes bibliographical references.
  ISBN 0-8423-3863-2
  1. Stepparents—United States. 2. Foster parents—United States.
3. Grandparents—United States. I. Title
HQ759.H87 1992
306.874—dc20
                                                    91-37808

Printed in the United States of America

99 98 97 96 95 94 93 92
 9   8   7   6   5   4   3   2

Loving someone else's child is like tending a field
Someone else plowed and planted.
You will weed, water, and work.
Someone else may harvest.
But you will have a part.

And while you love,
The fragile stalk will not be bent.
It will not be bruised.
It will not wither.
Because you were there,
It may grow tall.

—AEH

Contents

ONE
The Step-in Parent

William Haddad was an associate of [President John F.] Kennedy. After JFK was assassinated, his young son, John, asked Mr. Haddad, "Are you a daddy?" Haddad admitted that he was. Said little John, "Then will you throw me up in the air?"[1]

If you've picked this book up, you are probably faced with one of the greatest challenges of your life: loving someone else's child. Whether you are a step-parent, a foster parent, an adoptive parent, a grand-parent raising your grandchild, a legal guardian, or someone who wants to help a child on a part-time basis, this book is designed for you.

I had just settled into my usual chair at the check-in table for our Sunday school class when Tom approached. I was surprised that he'd venture into our madhouse of middle-schoolers, because he didn't have children in our class.

"Angie, I need to explain something," he said, bend-ing down to whisper. "You see, my niece, Wendy, has just moved in with us, and she's a troubled kid. I wanted to sign her up and let you know her story in case you have a problem with her in Sunday school."

I assured Tom that she'd be fine. (My husband has been a youth pastor for seventeen years, and I think he can handle almost anything.)

"Her parents kicked her out, and she's been making trouble at school. I just wanted to warn you in case she gives you a rough time here."

"It's okay, Tom. We'll keep an eye on her and try to make her feel welcome, so don't worry. She'll be okay."

Wendy was loitering in the hall, too timid to come into our bustling room until Tom went to get her. I handed her a visitor's card and motioned for Jaime, one of our super-friendly girls, to come over. Wendy filled out the card while Tom watched, his forehead creased in worry. Then Wendy found a seat in the crowd with Jaime.

"I don't know what I'm going to do," Tom confided. "My wife and I have never raised a teenage girl before. Suddenly, here she is. What are we supposed to do?"

Tom is one of an ever-increasing group of adults who find themselves raising someone else's child, and Wendy is one of many children who find themselves living in a home with at least one virtual stranger.

Loving someone else's child is one of the most difficult but potentially rewarding of all human relationships. If you are faced with this challenge, it is easy to throw up your hands in despair at each difficulty. But if you invest your time and effort, you and the child can succeed brilliantly in your newfound relationship by growing and learning together.

Whether you have become responsible for someone else's child through marriage, adoption, foster care, the extended family, or mere chance, you can succeed. Whether you are giving care and guidance to a child living in your home, or visiting on a part-time basis; whether the child lives with you for one month or ten years, your influence may change the direction of his or her life. And one life can change the world.

The father of the late Leonard Bernstein, the great American conductor and composer, was often criticized for not giving his talented son more encouragement when he was a child. "How was I to know he would grow up to be Leonard Bernstein?" his father protested.[2]

You don't know what God has in store for the child who needs you. But whether the child grows up to be a composer, an evangelist, or a fast-food burger flipper, he or she still deserves a loving home and all the encouragement you can give.

In this book you will find stories of people who have experienced struggle and calm, tears and joys, challenges and rewards as they loved other people's children. You will see that, whether or not they realize it, the first thing most people do is doff the description "someone *else's* child." "If I'm going to take this kid on," one father told me, "then he becomes *my kid*. It doesn't matter where he came from."

By the way, Tom's niece, Wendy, survived Sunday school and is doing well with her new family. Life with her uncle hasn't been perfect, but it's been a lot better than the life she knew before. Tom and his wife are making a difference.

Although this book is for anyone who is loving someone else's child, it has proved awkward to address every possible parenting situation consistently throughout the book. As I prepared to write this book, however, I came across an interesting scrap of information: the term *step* (as in "stepparent") comes from an Old English prefix meaning "bereaved." *Step* in its more common usage ("to step on the ladder") comes from an Old English word meaning "to stamp."

After mingling these two meanings, I've elected to call all people who love someone else's children *step-in* parents. I like the imagery. People who love someone else's children "step in" for a bereaved child and then "stamp" him with their influence, guidance, and love.

So for all of you who are stepping in where someone else has stepped out, three cheers! I hope you don't mind being called a step-in parent for the duration of this book. I intend it as a term of honor.

If God has brought a child into your life and you are filling the role of stepparent, guardian, godparent, teacher, coach, Big Brother, foster parent, grandparent, aunt, uncle, youth pastor, father figure, or friend, read on.

Loving Someone Else's Child could not have been written without the help of many families who either responded to questionnaires or submitted to interviews. To safeguard the privacy of these families, names and identifying characteristics have been changed.

TWO
Why Love Someone Else's Child?

Why love someone else's child? Because there are children who need you. Listen to these voices:

"Ten years ago, it was a shock to see a seven, eight, or nine-year-old come into the system, now it's not," says Danny Dawson, chief of the Orange-Osceola County State Attorney's juvenile division. "It's a trend."[1]

Glen Hester writes in *Child of Rage* of his personal experience growing up in a series of foster homes and institutions. He says he was bumped from foster homes to orphanages to institutions and, in the process, was severely abused. He tells how his being moved from place to place "destroyed my trust to the point that at age nine a psychiatrist diagnosed me as a child who neither loved nor trusted anyone."

"I feel," says Hester, "I was suffering from mental illness caused by my ill-fated experiences as a foster child." Hester credits his salvation from his rage, literally, to God. He says he is a born-again Christian.[2]

In March [1989], a mother went to buy drugs and left her one-year-old boy—who was dressed in a yellow designer jogging suit and expensive British Knights sneakers and wore a gold chain around his wrist—with two acquaintances, one of them an addict whose name the mother didn't know.

After the mother had been gone for four hours, the addict called the child protective services agency, but got impatient when no one came immediately. The woman left the child on a street corner, called police and said she found an abandoned boy on the way to the store. Police picked up the child, but were unable to locate the mother for two days. A source said the child was subsequently returned to his mother.[3]

The bad news is that 50 percent of all marriages end in divorce. The good news is that most of those people remarry.

Now for the real bad news: 65 percent of all second marriages end in divorce. And don't even ask about third, fourth, or fifth marriages. Those divorce statistics run even higher.[4]

An American child today is less likely to have a brother or sister than an American child in past decades, but is more likely to have a step-parent. . . . Professor Paul Glick of Arizona State

University finds it "reasonable to expect that one-third of the children now under eighteen have already experienced being a stepchild in a two-parent family or will do so before they reach the age of eighteen years."[5]

Current statistics indicate that 1,300 new stepfamilies are formed every day,[6] and that 6.8 million children under age eighteen live with a biological parent and a stepparent. Fifteen percent of all children in the United States who live with married parents live with a stepparent.[7]

THE AMERICAN FAMILY IS CHANGING

Why love someone else's child? Because the American family has eroded to the point where many children are not protected, nurtured, or wanted. Many other children, though we would like to believe they are much-loved, do not have secure homes. In previous generations most families wove cozy nests of security based on generations of togetherness. Grandparents laid a foundation, parents added a layer for stability, and like birds, all the elders gladly tore bits of themselves away so that the fledglings in the nest could have a cushion from which to start life.

I grew up in such a firm family. Every Thanksgiving we gathered at Aunt Irene's for turkey. Grandmother took each of us aside and quietly confided that *we* were her favorite grandchild. (We wised up, but we loved it anyway.) My older cousins invited me into their group—an honor. The younger cousins hung around together. The uncles sat in the den and watched bowl games; the women gathered in the kitchen and talked about womanly things. We took pictures and made home movies and swapped books and recipes and outgrown clothes.

Years have passed, but we still get together at Thanksgiving. We outgrew Aunt Irene's house long ago; now we rent a women's club in a small Florida town. My husband and I have driven fourteen hours from Virginia to make the annual reunion. Now we're closer, but we would try to make it if we lived in Alaska. In that meeting of turkey, casseroles, and cousins, there is continuity. We are a family.

Today my family is unusual. Although sociologists have long considered the family to be the social institution most resistant to change, over the last three decades the American family has undergone a remarkable transformation. Families today are smaller, farther apart geographically, and more isolated than in generations past. Divorce has cut family cords and weakened intergenerational ties. Children may not often see their siblings, much less their cousins.

Once the family nest is torn apart, it is not easily repaired. Families who seek to build new nests often find themselves without multigenerational support. Deep, unspoken bonds of love, trust, and respect cannot be magically called into place.

Nowhere is this more apparent than in blended families. Diane Mason recently attended the wedding of her stepdaughter, Laura, to George, a man with three children. As she looked over the crowd, she reflected on her family:

> Pretty soon the whole bunch of us would be related. A family that started in 1962, reshaped again in 1970 and again in 1979 is about to take another form again. Most of us aren't sure what to name our new relationships.
>
> My husband becomes, I suppose, a stepgrandfather. Which probably makes me a step-half-grandmother. My daughter, a half-aunt to George's children. My son, a half-uncle. George will be my step-son-in-law. He's fifteen years older than Laura, and I'm nine years younger than my husband, so George is only two years younger than me. I ask him not to call me Mom. George's sister and I decide to call ourselves step-half-sisters-in-law.[8]

Many factors, some benign and some malevolent, have combined to muddle the American family. People live longer today, and as a result they have more time to take advantage of the freedom of divorce. Divorce is simpler today, with "no-fault" allowances and societal acceptance. Drug abuse, sexual license, pornography, alcoholism, and hedonism all exert their influence over the fabric of American families.

Christian families are not immune to these influences. When Tom stopped by to register his niece in our Sunday school class, I wanted to tell him that she would not be the only child feeling quiet pain in a room of a hundred noisy middle-schoolers. Not a month passes without our learning of a Christian family in trouble. "My mom walked out on us last week," a kid will tell us. Or a mother will call and say, "Johnny has been embarrassed to come to church because his dad left. He doesn't want to face the other kids."

WE ARE TOO BUSY FOR CHILDREN

Kids need love, and in the middle of today's changes it takes a strong adult *who makes time* to provide that love.

In her book *Nobody's Children*, Valerie Bell tells of a kindergarten class assigned to invent machines to help with household problems. Many children invented robotic creations, but one little girl held a rectangular pillow to her head. Inside the pillow a tape recorder played back the voices of her parents. "I love you, Sarah!" her father crooned. "I'll be home soon, honey," her mother whispered.[9]

What was Sarah's "household problem"? She was lonely. Her parents weren't around as much as she needed them to be. Sarah has plenty of company—Hallmark Cards now markets greeting cards for parents who don't have time to spend with their children. "I wish I were there to tuck you in," says a card designed to be slipped under a pillow.[10]

Many children are overlooked. In the mad rush of our world, responsibility for children is often thrust upon whoever is willing to bear the burden—day-care providers, neighbors, even other children. "Children have just been a tremendous responsibility, especially for mothers," says Carl Storm, a professor of a marriage and family course at Lynchburg College. "And then you've got to consider the economic conditions. Historically, in an agricultural society, children were an asset. Today, they are a real liability."[11]

"Kids understand that they are being cheated out of childhood," says Yale psychology professor Edward Zigler. "Eight-year-olds are taking care of three-year-olds. We're seeing depression in children. We never thought we'd see that thirty-five years ago. There is a sense that adults don't care about them."[12]

WHERE ARE THE PARENTS?

It is not surprising that some children think adults don't care, when they rarely see their parents.

Many of these children are in foster care. The American foster-care system has its origins in the mid-nineteenth century, when the New York Children's Aid Society began sending street kids to midwestern farm families. Today it is a bureaucratic system of social-service agencies run by states and local communities under federal guidelines. Sixty-one percent of children in foster care are taken from their parents because of abuse and neglect.[13]

The American system of foster care is designed to protect children, but it often harms them unintentionally. Children flourish in a loving foster home, but every time a child is moved, he loses his ability to bond with and trust a new family.

This inability to form attachments is breeding personality disorders in American children. "More than half of all troubled children we see in our practice have a history of being shuffled and bounced about," says Foster Cline, an authority on unattached children, who runs a mental health clinic in Evergreen, Colorado.[14]

Other children spend more time with caregivers than with their parents. American grandparents, for example, are being called upon in record numbers to care for their grandchildren. Men and women who knew by instinct how to raise their own young are now being offered classes in the latest child-rearing techniques.

"A lot of the mothers work now," says Norma Bock, director of maternity services at Nazareth Hospital. "It's the grandparents that are the caregivers."[15]

CHILDREN ARE NOT VALUED

A Filipino family lives in my neighborhood. It includes an older woman and her four grown children—a daughter and three sons—plus the daughter's young son. Several family members are still in the Philippines, waiting for an immigration visa.

I've watched the family with interest. They work as a team. The daughter, a nurse, tries to round up clients for her brother, a dentist. Another brother is up early every morning, studying computer science in the quiet of his back porch, and in the afternoons he helps watch the baby. The younger brother lives at college during the week but comes home every weekend to be with his family and help at the house. Those who haven't earned their American citizenship are working hard for it, and that, too, is a team effort.

In the middle of it all is eighteen-month-old Steven. Someone is always there to care for him: his grandmother, an uncle, his mother. When I'm outside in the early evening I can hear grandma singing "The Star Spangled Banner" and Steven singing it right along with her.

I've noticed what my neighbors value: citizenship, family togetherness, hard work, education, and Steven. Steven's father is still in the Philippines, but the child has never lacked for loving attention. He is a part of the family team, and as such, he is valued.

Most of us have adopted a different set of values today. We value relaxation, pleasure, convenience, privacy. We see ourselves as distinct islands, connected to our extended families by the slenderest of threads. We are so busy making and being and doing that we have neglected to value our elders and our children.

CHILDREN ARE AT RISK

Why love someone else's child? Because love and attention can save a child at risk.

According to a recent analysis of a nationwide survey conducted in 1988, researchers for the National Center for Health Statistics found a remarkably high incidence of emotional and academic problems among children living in single-parent families and stepfamilies. The investigators interpreted "the alarmingly high prevalence of emotional and behavioral problems among today's children" as ample justification for public concerns about the increasing number of U.S. children being raised in "something other than harmonious two-parent families."[16]

Children from these "something other" families are

more vulnerable to teenage pregnancy, drug abuse, behavioral problems, and even learning disabilities. Others are more prone to violence, committing heinous crimes without a shred of remorse. Teenage murderers are not uncommon today: 1,311 people under age eighteen were charged with murder in 1986. One of them was a jealous twelve-year-old who killed his mother and younger sister over birthday party plans.

Many experts believe that most violent children are products of shattered family relationships. "Almost all violent children have suffered a break in their attachment to others," says Carole McKelvey, coauthor of *High Risk: Children without a Conscience.*[17]

CHILDREN'S ISOLATION IS INCREASING

Why love someone else's child? Because if our society continues along its present track, children will soon be even more isolated, responsible to and for themselves. Because of overworking parents and multi-family groups, many children will learn to depend upon themselves alone, not on caring adults. Joint-custody arrangements, in which children divide their time between their divorced parents, will increase. Children will make their own decisions about their friends, their schools, and how they spend their time.

Fifty years from now, predict some specialists in family law, it will be common for children to have their own attorneys present at divorce hearings. In the future, children as young as twelve will be routinely allowed to choose the parent they will live with after the divorce.[18]

Other aspects of future family life are also alarming. The age at which men and women are marrying for the first time has been steadily rising since the 1960s. These families are waiting longer to have children while they pursue educational and career goals, and once the children are born, parents are more likely than ever to continue in the work force. The Bureau of Labor Statistics reports that in the last decade the labor force participation rate for women with very young children (under three years old) has increased from one-third to one-half.

Where are these children while their parents are working? Parents are moving away from using care in the child's home to using group-care arrangements such as those of day-care centers and nursery schools. Between 1982 and 1985, the percentage of mothers employed full-time who used organized child care for children younger than five rose from 20 percent to 30 percent.[19] Who will give these children the emotional support they need if their parents are gone for ten or twelve hours a day? An overworked nursery school teacher?

Even television reflects the lack of parental role models for children. The traditional family, where Dad and Mom nurture and take responsibility for the children, is nearly absent from weekly television programs. With the notable exception of "The Cosby Show" and one or two others, children on television are usually advised and guided by butlers, housekeepers, aliens, grandparents, neighbors, coaches, and friends.

Why love someone else's child? Because so many of

today's children do not have cozy family nests. They have Nintendo; they have "home alone" security systems; they have television, radio, and microwave dinners. But often they do not have an adult to love and guide them.

PASSING THE FLAG OF TRUTH

Why love someone else's child? Perhaps one of the best reasons for agreeing to be a step-in parent is to "pass the flag of truth," as Edith Schaeffer describes it:

> The truth was meant to be given from generation to generation. If those who knew God and who had so very much to tell about Him had always been faithful, and had always stuck to the commands or the rules of the relay, there would have been no gaps. Each generation would have learned from the one before. Fathers and mothers were to tell sons and daughters. There was supposed to be a perpetual relay of truth without a break. . . .
>
> Consider your place in the family as central, not just in this moment of history, but as part of the "relay." Don't let a gap come because of you. Don't take the beauty of the family life—and the reality of being able to hand down true truth to one more generation—as a light thing. It is one of the central commands of God. It is direct disobedience to God to *not* make known His truth, to *not* make known the truth of Himself, and to *not* make known the wonderful works that He has done. It is

> not a responsibility to be handed over to the
> church and Sunday school. . . .
>
> One person in one family in one village in one
> county in one nation can, even *alone*, be the one
> to start the beginning of a new line of believers,
> as that one begins to really pray for specific indi-
> viduals, to talk when the moment opens up, and
> to lead a few others one by one to know true
> truth.[20]

What does God expect you to do with someone
else's child? His admonitions are the same for all who
raise children, whether or not they are biologically
related. In fact, the Bible contains many examples of
men and women who raised other people's children:
Mordecai raised his niece, Esther, who became queen
of Persia; the Pharaoh's daughter raised Moses, leader
of the Israelites; and Joseph the carpenter raised
Jesus, the son who was not related to him biologically.

As parents or step-in parents, we are to teach children the commandments and principles of God's Word:

> These commandments that I give you today are
> to be upon your hearts. Impress them on your
> children. Talk about them when you sit at home
> and when you walk along the road, when you lie
> down and when you get up (Deuteronomy 6:6-7).

> Train a child in the way he should go, and when
> he is old he will not turn from it (Proverbs 22:6).

Marilee Kastle, a foster mother to two children,
says that she wants to give her foster children a solid
background in biblical training. "We find the church

a big help as it gives us a place to turn to when we get discouraged," she says. "The children love to go to Sunday school and generally do not miss a Sunday. We are trying to give them a solid foundation so that whatever happens, they have a biblical knowledge to fall back on."

"I have poor health," says sixty-five-year-old Mel Atkins, who is raising his two grandchildren, ages eight and nine, "and over my lifetime a lot of things have happened to me so I should have been dead a long time ago. But I keep surviving and I always wondered why, until this situation came along. I feel that taking care of these children is why God has me here.

"We go to a Lutheran church and try to give them a religious upbringing. We say our prayers, no matter where we are. My wife and I try to set good examples and try to expose them to things that we feel are spiritual. I just feel it's what God wants me to do. My wife and I had only been married eighteen months before the children were thrust upon us, but we adopted them and we're grateful God gave us a chance to do this."

"YOU HAVE DONE IT UNTO ME"

Last night I dismissed my class of eighth-grade girls and stood out in the hall waiting for my husband, who seemed to be involved in a serious counseling session. When Gary finally came out, I couldn't help noticing that his eyes were red. He drew a deep breath and shook his head slowly.

"What's wrong?" I asked. "That was Jenny, right?"

"She's been through three divorces," Gary said simply. "Her mother's hurting right now, and Jenny doesn't know who she can talk to. She's mixed up and confused and lonely."

Why should you love someone else's child? Because at any given time, God might bring you into a child's life when *you* are the only one who can give what that child needs. Whether you fill that role as a counselor, stepparent, grandparent, friend, teacher, coach, Big Brother, aunt, uncle, godparent, guardian, neighbor, or foster parent, you can make a difference.

Why love someone else's child? Because "whatever you did for one of the least of these," Jesus told us, "you did for me" (Matt. 25:40).

THREE
Who Loves Other People's Children?

On Mother's Day last year, I noticed that our church's traditional recognition of mothers had gained a few twists. We still gave little gifts to the oldest mother and the mother with the most children, but we also recognized the single mother with the most children and the woman with the most great-grandchildren.

It was the woman with thirty-two great-grandchildren who caught my attention. I was expecting an eighty-year-old woman to come down the aisle, but instead a chipper woman who didn't look a day over forty-five claimed the prize. I later found out that she has thirty-two great-grandchildren through a blended family.

No matter where you look today, all kinds of people at all ages are learning to love other people's children: stepparents, grandparents, adoptive parents, foster parents, godparents, guardians, and other surrogates. Each type of step-in parent has distinct challenges, so we will look at each group separately. But all share the common joys and frustrations of loving someone else's child, so I recommend that you read this whole chapter, even the sections that don't specifically discuss your situation.

STEPPARENTS

Some demographers predict that as many as a third of all children born in the 1980s may live with a stepparent before they are eighteen. According to the latest available census figures, there were close to 7 million children living in stepfamilies in 1985, an increase of 11.6 percent in just five years. "Most people have a personal connection with a stepfamily," University of Pennsylvania sociologist Frank Furstenberg told *Newsweek* magazine. "If it's not their parents, it's their child or their grandparents or their husband's parents."[1]

Children living in stepfamilies have more than their share of difficulties adjusting to new situations. Not only do they undergo the pain of divorce and the trauma of splitting one family unit, they must also make adjustments when the family changes to include additional family members—through a parent's remarriage, for instance.[2] Even though a new family, with a mother and father, is formed, it is important to understand that the traditional family has not been reinstated. "One of the consistent findings in research is that stepparenthood does not re-create the nuclear family," says Furstenberg. "It does not put the family back together again."[3]

With each additional change in the family, a child's

trauma can be magnified. Children feel pangs of adjustment when another baby is born or brought into the family, and if this subsequent family breaks in divorce, all family members are drastically affected. Successful stepfamilies recognize the risks of change. They work toward lessening the negative influences and strengthening the positive.

More and more people today find themselves with an instant family, saying "I do" to more than just a spouse—to the kids, the in-laws, and the family pets, too. Nearly two out of three remarriages today involve children from a previous marriage,[4] and many newly married couples find that the word stepfamily brings more than they bargained for.

There are negative connotations simply to the word *step.* What did Cinderella, Snow White, Hansel and Gretel, and a host of other fairy-tale characters have in common? A wicked stepmother! Why do some people introduce the kids in the household by saying, "So-and-so is my stepson, but this is my *real* daughter"? Is the stepson artificial? Is he not real, too?

Many families avoid the use of *step,* preferring to hide the fact that a stepfamily relationship exists. But the fact cannot be denied. Whether the family is "blended," "reconstituted," or "united," stepfamilies are fundamentally different from other families. "We've never interacted like my ideal of a nuclear family," says Mark Bruce Rosin, a stepfather. "We've always interacted as just what we are: a stepfamily."[5]

"Stepfathering is not at all like parenting, which surprised me," said one stepfather. "It's more like being a scout leader."[6]

When stepfamilies first form, too often the parents expect a honeymoon. The teenage daughter may like Dad's girlfriend just fine while they're dating, but when she becomes "Mom," look out! Or a son, who's been protecting his mother, may resent having that role taken from him by her new husband. And once the marriage vows are spoken, the child's dream that Mom and Dad will reconcile and reunite is forever gone. It doesn't take long for the honeymoon to shift to shocking reality.

Stepparenting used to be fairly unusual, novel enough to be interesting in old movies such as *Yours, Mine and Ours,* and television shows such as "The Brady Bunch." We laughed at the situations these people encountered, and all problems were resolved through a heart-to-heart talk over a cup of coffee.

But real life isn't "The Brady Bunch." A friend of mine who is a middle school counselor told me, "The kids all tell me they want their families to be like the Waltons. Everyone wants the Waltons, but *nobody* has it."

The details of stepfamily life are discussed throughout this book, but here are some "nutshell" principles particularly for stepfamilies. Many of them will sound familiar to other kinds of step-in families as well.

Don't expect "The Brady Bunch." When representatives from two or more fractured families come together, the result is not a beautifully blended bunch. While everyone may unite in principle, it's the little things that stall the weaving of a new family fabric: How much allowance do the kids get? How does the family spend Christmas? What television shows do the kids watch?

Christian families may not have superior abilities to cope with the situation. "Christian families often have more emotional fallout than other families," one parent told me. "Divorce brings with it embarrassment, an extra burden of guilt, and a sense of failure."

It's possible to carry the burden of guilt and failure into a second marriage, so blended families have to be careful to evaluate what is really important.

Sally Mears keenly felt the eyes of the Christian community on her when she married Henry, a pastor with two children ages four and seven. "It was difficult being a minister's wife," she says, "because women wouldn't hesitate to tell me that I could never love the stepchildren as much as I would love my own."

"When I got married, I wanted to love the kids like they were mine, and I expected that they would love me like their real mother. I thought we'd live an idealistic fairy tale and be a happy family, and it wouldn't matter who their real mother was. The kids had accepted me and were excited about us getting married, so I thought everything would be great."

Expectations may have to be adjusted. The Mears family's honeymoon faded to reality over simple issues like food:

"I'm not going to eat that."

"Yes, you are. You'll stay there until you try it."

"That's yucky. I hate it."

Yet despite the occasional battles of the will, Sally was happy. "I felt I was providing a stable, loving environment for them," she says. "They were part of a loving, two-parent family. We were picking up the pieces of the past and going forward together."

Expect outside influences. A stepfamily is not a nuclear family. It has ties to other people that cannot be broken, and it has no history or sense of past togetherness to anchor it through rough times. In addition, stepfamily members may have obligations to people outside the immediate family.

After her marriage, Sally had to cope with intrusive telephone calls from the children's biological mother. The woman told her children bizarre stories, and when Sally had a baby, the ex-wife told them that Sally would never love them as much as she loved the new baby because they were not blood relations.

Be prepared for change. When Henry's oldest child was thirteen, she came to Sally and Henry and announced that she wanted to go live with her mother. "That was the hardest thing to deal with," Sally recalls. "My dream of us being a family was shattered. I thought the kids didn't like me, that everything I did was wrong. I was hurt, but my husband was hurt, too, and I ached at the thought that his child wanted to leave."

Be willing to sacrifice for the common good. When different families come together, they bring different values, different notions of spirituality, different traditions, and different physical belongings. Steve Newton, who married his wife, Elaine, in 1986, expected that living with her twelve- and fourteen-year-old sons would be easy. "I expected them to do everything the way I wanted it done, to have my values, and not to question my authority," he says. "It turned out that all those expectations were incorrect.

"The hardest thing about loving someone else's

child," says Steve, "is melding my expectations and
ways of doing things with theirs. They were comfortable with doing things the way their mom did things.
They had traditions: they liked camping and bluegrass
concerts; every summer they traveled to visit relatives; but now that we were a family some things
changed."

Define love as commitment, not feelings. Some family
counselors tell stepparents not to be concerned if
they don't want to love someone else's child. But
civility is a weak bonding agent.

Steve was wise enough to realize that feelings of
love for the boys wouldn't come overnight. "I was in
love with my wife in every way, and I accepted the
children as part of her. I made the decision to love
them because I believe love is a commitment of the
will. I decided to commit my time and resources, and
to be a parent—and that was a harder decision than
simply letting Elaine parent them. But the feeling of
love came later. I felt myself loving them within six
months to a year; and I knew they loved me the same
way within a year or two."

*Expect to have authority over the children in your
own home.* Stepparents must be free to enforce house
rules, and their authority should be respected. But,
as one parent pointed out, if the child's biological
mother or father continues a nurturing, active role in
the child's life, the stepparent should not attempt to
usurp that role. Though you should expect to have
authority in your home, don't expect undivided loyalty. Give your child the freedom to love his absent
parent.

Give everyone—including yourself—time to adjust.
Bob and Sherrie Williams met and married in 1972.
Bob had six kids; Sherrie had three. Three of Bob's
boys joined Sherrie's three girls in the household.

Bob had been alone with his six kids for two years,
a lonely man up until two o'clock in the morning
each night doing laundry and keeping his house in
order. It was hard for both Bob and Sherrie to give up
the dual roles of mother/father they had been filling.
It took Bob and Sherrie about a year to relax in their
new roles. When their new baby, Gaylyn, was born,
Bob and Sherrie finally felt "cemented" in their
responsibilities.

Expect children to be torn between parents. Children
often feel angry or torn by conflicting loyalties.
When presented with a stepparent, they need help
understanding that this person will not replace a
biological parent, but can provide a special, loving
relationship.

Sherrie had problems filling her role as a stepmother. The boys' mother was alive and frequently
meddled in family affairs. She told the boys not to
call Sherrie "Mom," referring to her instead as "the
other woman."

Bob noticed that the girls tended to be defiant
toward him at first. "I felt they had a hard time accept-
ing me because they lost their father," he says. "For a
while I really felt on the out."

*Expect that children may be angry over the lack of
control in their lives. Learn to recognize displaced
anger.* Psychologist Patricia Papernow, a stepfamily
specialist, warns parents not to overlook a child's

sense of loss. "If you find a family that's 'blended,' someone got creamed," she says. The adults who visualize a "happily ever after" with a new family may not realize that their children were hoping for a reconciliation of the old.[7]

Angry children may act out their feelings at school rather than at home, or they may focus their anger on the person they can most afford to lose—the stepparent. Adults can help children verbalize these confusing feelings by asking questions to untangle the ball of anger: "Why are you mad at Sue? Are you afraid you won't see your mom again? Are you upset because you have to share your room?"

Stress your commitment to each other. One evening not long after their marriage, Bob and Sherrie argued at the dinner table. The kids grew quiet; then nine-year-old Peter burst into tears: "Mom said you'd fight and then you'd get a divorce!"

Sherrie looked at the boy and then looked at Bob. She yelled: "I wouldn't give him the satisfaction of a divorce!" The tension broke, and the kids laughed.

"They were insecure," Sherrie recalls, "and they had to see that couples can disagree without getting a divorce. We had to build up their security."

Bob and Sherrie Williams today are a well-cemented family of ten children and sixteen grandchildren. "We have a special family because we consider them all ours," says Sherrie. "Gaylyn is the only child still at home, but all our other kids come over at least once a week—a lot of people are jealous of our togetherness. God's been the center of our family, and he's made a big difference."

Sherrie smiles. "There were rough times, but everybody has rough times. You just pull yourself through them with God's help. That's what family is all about."

SHORT-TERM PARENTS

Perhaps you act as a step-in parent only for brief periods, when your spouse's children come to visit or when nieces or nephews come for an extended stay. How can you be a positive influence on a child that simply visits? How can you help this "drop-in" child feel comfortable in your home?

Emily and John Visher stress putting yourself in the child's place. Visiting children usually feel like outsiders or intruders in the family and the neighborhood. It is helpful if they have some place in the house that is their own, such as a drawer or a shelf for toys or clothes. The Vishers suggest including visiting children in family chores and projects to make them feel more a part of the group.[8]

Sally Mears's two stepchildren visit occasionally during the summer. The boy seems to feel right at home, but the girl enjoys bringing a friend for her one- or two-week stays.

Some children enjoy looking forward to a special traditional activity during their visit: a vacation, a game of Monopoly, a cookout, or a picnic. Perhaps you could establish traditions of "welcome home" meals or a child's favorite dessert. Even though you have this child with you for only a short period, you can still establish meaningful, consistent traditions and patterns. Aim to make his short time with you a predictable, stable element of his life.

GRANDPARENTS RAISING GRANDCHILDREN

Mel Atkins suspected that his daughter and her husband had a drug problem. He didn't know for sure, but he was concerned because the couple lived in subsidized housing and never had food in the house for their young children. "I'd take them food and dishes," he says, "but when I visited again, everything would be gone. So finally I got permission to take the kids. My daughter wanted a divorce, so we paid her legal fees and set her up in an apartment, but when the rent ran out, she sold everything and disappeared. I haven't seen or talked to her in over six years."

Mel and his wife, Phyllis, are raising their two grandchildren, whom they have adopted. "They're our children, we love them, and we're very protective of them," Mel says. "They're going to have to deal with old crotchety grandparents bringing them up," he laughs, "but I try to participate in everything. I'm retiring, so I'll have more time to go to their swimming meets, ballet recitals, and soccer games."

Phyllis started a group called Grandparents Raising Grandchildren at their church in Clayton, Missouri. "At this point, we don't quite relate with the problems of the group," Mel says. "A lot of those folks are still in the traumatic stage where something horrendous is happening. It's pathetic to see some things loving grandparents go through, but most of them are loving people who care more about their grandchildren than their children do."

Mel and Phyllis have adjusted well to raising their grandchildren, who are now eight and nine. Do they keep Mel young? "They keep me tired!" Mel chuckles. "But everything's working out. And if you want to use my real name, go right ahead. I'm proud of what my family is."

Today, more than ever, many children need their grandparents' attention full-time. According to *Time* magazine, 3 million children live with their grandparents, a 50 percent increase over the past decade.[9]

Ray LaMotte, director of news media for the Los Angeles County Department of Children's Services, told the *Los Angeles Times* that relatives are the first choice of placement for abused or neglected children. "The type of relative isn't specified," he said, "but we know that the majority are grandparents."[10]

Grandparents who had planned to spend their golden years traveling or in quiet relaxation are often surprised to find their grandchildren on their doorstep for an indefinite stay. Most grandparents take in their grandchildren rather than see the kids go into foster care. But underneath their willingness, there is often an undercurrent of anger. A study of a group of parenting grandparents found that many of them resented the children who had not been able to be good parents.[11]

"One of the biggest problems the grandparents have is with the natural parents," says Mignon Scherer, who is raising her grandson. She started a support group in San Diego with other grandparents rearing grandchildren. "Many grandparents are fearful of their children. . . . They make threats." Along with the usual hassles of child rearing, then, grandparents also face grief, depression, anger, guilt, confusion, and anxiety over their grown children.[12]

Barbara Holmes told *Newsday*, "I love my grandchildren. They are my babies. But I feel tired. I get angry. I get stressed. I get resentful when I've had a long day, when nothing's going right. I feel it's wrong for a person, having raised her own children, then to have to take on the responsibility of raising someone else's children, unless those people are dead."[13]

Children are placed with grandparents for many reasons, including neglect, permanent or temporary abandonment, involvement with drugs or alcohol, physical or sexual abuse, mental illness, and incarceration. Additionally, many grandparents find themselves raising their grandchildren while an adult child who lives with them works all day. They may not have legal custody of the child, but for all practical purposes, they are fulfilling parental roles in the child's life.

Kids who live with their grandparents like being kept in the family, but many feel insecure. They know their grandparents are older, and they may worry about grandparents becoming ill or dying—who would take care of them then? Many kids feel resentful because their grandparents are unable to participate in active ventures.

Grandparents, too, find that things are different when the grandkids are underfoot twenty-four hours a day. "We had just learned to play golf," said Albert Johnson, sixty-six, to the *Los Angeles Times*, "and now my wife can join me only about twice a year." He and his wife are rearing their grandchildren, a nine-year-old girl and an eight-year-old boy.[14]

Financial resources, carefully planned to last a household of two through retirement, may be strained when stretched to meet the expenses of raising a child. Patience, energy, and wisdom are demanded as well. The child-rearing rules of the fifties have to be broadened. Today's kids know about sex, divorce, abuse, loneliness, nuclear war, and fear.

Fortunately, grandparents have seen it all. They have experience, wisdom, and lots of love. "Being a grandparent," says Darnell White, "is like having a second chance in life. Along with our grandchildren, we can be young all over again."[15]

"Our grandchildren bring joy to our lives just as our own children did," says Mignon Scherer. "Maybe more so, because we're mellower and we know what we're doing. We may have other problems, health problems, not as much money, a loss of freedom. Still, it's like a gift. You can't feel too sad with little kids around."[16]

ADOPTIVE PARENTS

You may be thinking that adoption isn't quite the same as loving someone else's child, and I agree. When you adopt a child, whether he is a stepchild or completely new to your family, that child becomes your own and not someone else's. My husband and I have adopted two children, and if anyone were to suggest they weren't mine, I'd raise a fuss.

But there is a time when prospective adoptive

parents wonder about loving someone else's child. What will it be like to bring a biological stranger into the household? Will this child feel like one of the family? Will he or she be accepted? Will the love for an adopted child be different from the love for a biological child? What if he or she has special needs we cannot fill?

Over the years I've had the chance to talk to several adoptive parents about their reasons for loving someone else's child and choosing to make that child their own. Buddy and Anna White of Washington State found that some of their family members were cautious about adoption. "We were the first ones to use this new way of forming a family," says Anna. "But their hesitation disappeared completely when there was a person to love!" Jeane, now eight, joined the family through a privately arranged adoption when she was two days old.

"The biggest challenge of adoption is getting through the maze to the child," says Anna. "Once you're there, one of the primary challenges is to keep a balance among the adoption triangle of the birth parents, the adoptive parents, and the child."

The Whites balance the triangle by telling their daughter that her birth parents gave her life and a birthday; they are giving her a family.

In New York, Bill and Gia McGibbon are expecting their second child. Their three-year-old, Gaby, came on the wings of a 747 from Korea, and their newest arrival will come from India. Where the children originate isn't important; as far as Bill and Gia are concerned, these children came on the wings of prayer.

"I had been wanting to do this long before I got married," says Gia. "And when we learned that we were infertile, it seemed even more like God's plan for us.

"Adoption is a very scriptural thing. We explained Gaby's adoption by telling her she's adopted by us just like God adopts each one of us. We have a record album with a song about how God had only one son, but he wanted more, so we're adopted by the King."

Gia describes an international adoption as a miracle on top of the original miracle of birth. "Only the Lord can see everything and put all the pieces together," she says.

Wanda and Paul Peters of Florida have two children: Marcie, four, and Millie, three. Both were adopted as infants through a local private agency.

"We were going to a fertility specialist and we did everything short of in vitro fertilization," recalls Wanda. "We wanted to have children very badly. The waiting lists for adoption agencies where we lived averaged between five and seven years."

The Peters invested twelve years in the search for a child before they became parents, but Wanda is glad they chose to complete their family through adoption. "The greatest challenge of adoptive parenting is to assure them that their birth parents did love them and that we love them just as much as we would love a biological child."

Donald and Joyce Smithson of Washington state have four children: Donald, 26; Mary, 21: Ronnie, 15; and Crissy, 14. The youngest three were added by adoption.

"We had never considered adoption until our

minister called one night and asked if I wanted a baby," says Joyce. "I thought he wanted me to baby-sit, and I said I had a house full of company. Then he explained that he was asking if I wanted to *have* a baby!"

The Smithsons went to the hospital to see the three-pound baby in the hospital incubator. After their first look at her, they knew she was meant for them.

Ten years later the Smithson family added two biological siblings, ages three and four. Ronnie and Crissy had lived in twelve different foster homes. They had known physical and mental abuse. Someone had beaten the little boy's nose totally flat; someone else had set both children's feet on fire. After two years with the Smithsons, the children were free for adoption and the court officially recognized what the Smithsons had known all along: Ronnie and Crissy had come home to stay.

It was difficult to heal the hurts of the past, but Joyce and Donald were determined that these two children would be loved to health. "Today people cannot believe they came from that kind of background," says Joyce. "Ronnie is funny and delightful, and they are loving and nurturing to other kids. When they have a problem now, it's a normal problem. When you adopt an older child, you never can erase their past, but they can grow stronger from it."

Alvin and Denise Knutson live in Idaho with their large family. Denise had originally thought she would like a large family with both adoptive and biological children, but the Knutsons suffered through six miscarriages while they were adopting six children:

Edward, 21; Marcie, 19; Somer, 18; Thomas, 18; Rick, 15; and Becky, 14.

Denise is honest about her family's experience: they have had lots of challenges, and they've needed a lot of prayer. Among the problems she has encountered are a child running away, bad language, drugs, sex, and alcohol. "But we have the joy of seeing that God is faithful and that his plans work together for good. Sometimes the things that appear to be the most terrible have wonderful solutions."

The Knutson children were adopted at various ages ranging from three to fourteen. For those considering adopting an older child, Denise advises: "Make sure you have a good support system. We have our parents living next door, and our church body has saved our lives over and over again."

Ruth and Arnold Hernandez are biracial, as are all their nine children. Five of the children are adopted, and the family is hoping for new arrivals.

The best thing about adoption for Ruth is parenting. "I just like being a mom," she says. In 1980 she and her husband, with their three-month-old baby in arms, went to an agency and announced: "We want a large family. We don't care if the kids fell from Mars. How many can you give us and how soon?"

The social workers thought they were crazy, of course, but eventually Ruth and Arnold learned about the Purchase of Services program for hard-to-place children. These children can be adopted from private agencies, and the federal government reimburses many adoption expenses including, in some cases, air fares, car rental, and adoption fees. Often the families are granted a monthly subsidy payment. "The program varies from state to state," Ruth explains, "but basically the government has realized that adoption is cheaper than keeping a child in foster care indefinitely."

Ruth notes that the best pool of prospective adoptive applicants is religious people who live their faith, especially people who are middle class or lower middle class. "There are a lot of people out there with big hearts and small checkbooks," she says.

Mary Ann Kuharski has thirteen children, six of whom are adopted. Her children come from Cambodia, Vietnam, the Philippines, India, and Mexico. Why did she adopt? "An inner tug on a corner of our hearts always seemed to lead us onward in pursuit of just one more," she says. Would she recommend adoption to others? "Only to those couples who are willing to accept the middle-of-the-night wakings, the tantrums and tears, the obstacles and unknowns, and the heart-tugging exhilaration that can only come with the gift of love. Disappointments there will be, but our six imports and seven 'tummy' children have given us more joy, more love, and more faith than we ever would have dreamed possible. We're so grateful for those six little hearts that were waiting to be matched. Adoption is indeed a privilege."[17]

FOSTER PARENTS

In 1990, over 360,000 American children were removed from their homes and placed in foster care. With the number of child abuse, neglect, and drug-addiction cases increasing yearly, the need for foster families is growing.

When Nick and Joan Granitsas volunteered to be foster parents, they thought children would arrive with a suitcase of clean clothes and a bicycle. But when their first foster children arrived—a four-year-old girl, a seven-year-old boy, and a twelve-year-old girl—they were filthy. The two youngest had head lice, and the seven-year-old drooled and couldn't speak intelligibly.

Joan admitted to *Christian Parenting Today* that fostering a child is not like making him a part of the permanent family. "Saying good-bye is almost like a death," she says, "but the Lord lets us have a respite before we take in another child. You have to consider foster care as a ministry to the natural family—one of reuniting a family unit. You shouldn't look at foster care to add to your own family."

Joan and Nick have been fostering children for sixteen years, and they want to continue. "We want to be a temporary respite for kids whose families are in crisis," explains Joan. "Even a kid in trouble deserves a family to love him."[18]

Tom Behrens, director of the Northside Ecumenical Night Ministry in Chicago, encourages church families to open their homes to teenagers who need emergency shelter. "Churches offer sanctuary to Latin American refugees; why not sanctuary for our kids?" he asks. Since October 1987, when the Exodus Homes project began operating, families have been providing emergency shelter until youngsters can move back with their parents or find appropriate care.

Several families have been licensed by the state to

provide foster care, and support groups from several area congregations have been trained to learn why youngsters become homeless and what kinds of problems they face on the streets: drugs, alcohol, prostitution, and AIDS. "The entire congregation becomes invested in that kid and his or her welfare," explains Paul Henderson, the project coordinator.[19]

Recently I ran into a couple from my church at a local bookstore. They had children in our youth department, and they were bubbling over with excitement about their latest family venture: foster parenting.

"We had been waiting until our kids were old enough not to feel jealous," the wife explained. "And now our kids are really excited about this."

Why did they want to be foster parents? "There is such a need," the husband said. "We heard about all the crack babies, babies damaged by alcohol, and failure-to-thrive babies, so we decided we wanted to take care of the little ones who need special help."

This couple reminded me of an urgent need in our country today. According to the National Association for Perinatal Addiction Research and Education, about one out of every ten newborns in the United States—375,000 a year—is exposed in the womb to illegal and dangerous drugs. In major cities, many hospitals report that at least one out of five newborns shows the effects of drugs.

Foster homes for drug-affected infants are in short supply. These infants need special care and trained caregivers. *Time* magazine reports that in New York City annual placements of drug-affected babies run to

3,500, compared with 750 before the widespread use of crack cocaine which began in the mid 1980s.[20]

A friend of mine, an obstetrical nurse, once told me about the surprising number of crack babies she has helped deliver. "I wish we could send them all to foster homes," she said, "but because there's a shortage of foster homes, they usually end up back with their drug-addicted mothers."

"Christians ought to get involved in foster care," Joe Maddox, a foster father, told me. "If anyone ought to do it, we ought to. You know who gave the biggest Christmas party for the foster kids in our city?"

I shook my head.

He told me about a cult group that had given every foster child in our city a present. "The cults don't hesitate to reach out to those kids," he said. "So why do we?"

GODPARENTS AND GUARDIANS

I don't have godparents and you may not either. Traditionally, a godparent's responsibility was to ensure a child's religious training. Many denominations do not appoint godparents, and in the ones that do, the role is often only ceremonial. The only time I hear much about godparents is when the royal Windsors of England name seven or eight people as godparents for the latest royal baby.

Yet many today feel a new role exists for godparents. "In an era when families break up or move frequently, godparents can provide love and stability to their godchildren," says Gerard Austin, professor of theology at the Catholic University of America.[21]

Committed godparents take the child seriously and maintain close contact through the years. They are understanding, patient, and good role models. They stand ready to fill needs the parents can't meet.

Similar to the role of godparent is the role of guardian. The Scriptures tell us that Job acted as guardian to fatherless children (Job 29:12, 16). He did not adopt them legally, but he took up their cases and provided for them.

Legally, a guardian is a person invested with the power and charged with the duty of taking care of another person. The guardian manages the property and rights of a person who lacks age, understanding, or self-control, or is incapable of conducting his affairs.

Foster parenting is one type of guardianship. Foster parents take in needy children temporarily until the children can be reunited with their families, although legal custody remains with the social services department that does the placement.

You may be acting as an informal "foster parent" or guardian for a niece or nephew. In our church's youth department, we often meet kids who are living for a limited time—often a year—with an aunt or uncle, an older brother or sister, or even a grandparent. These family placements are made because the child's biological parents are having problems; they wish to remove their child from a negative peer group; or the parents are called away for some reason such as military duty, job training, or education.

If you have drawn up a will, you have probably named a guardian for your children in the event of your death. Incidentally, it is very important that you do this. If something were to happen to you and your spouse and you did not have a will, there is no guarantee that your children would be placed with the people you would have chosen to raise them. If you do not have a legal will, consider this issue immediately, pray about it, and arrange to name a responsible, godly guardian for your children should the need arise.

OTHER PARENTAL SURROGATES

Timmy sat alone crying in the back of his elementary school classroom. Bob Kennedy, a volunteer in the Generations Together program of the Pennsylvania school, went up and talked to the boy. Timmy's father had walked out on the family the day before, but Timmy only remarked that he didn't have any friends.

"I can be your friend," Kennedy told Timmy. And so began a friendship that has lasted for years.

With our country's mobility, dispersed families, and high divorce rate, huge numbers of children are deprived of the special kind of attention they would have received from grandparents. The Generations Together program in Pennsylvania is just one of many programs geared to join lonely children with senior adults.[22]

At a day-care center in downtown Pittsburgh, four older women rock, fuss over, feed, and change babies. At a school for exceptional children, elders help care for mentally retarded, physically disabled, and emotionally troubled children. Together, the old and the young fill needs in each other's lives. The children get lots of attention and a listening ear, and the elders find a routine, pleasant interaction with children—and lots of appreciative hugs. Both groups leave feeling good about themselves.

The erosion of family life is creating new opportunities for many people to love someone else's children. Scholars at the National Center for Education Statistics and the U.S. Department of Education complained that "all too frequently teachers must serve as 'parent surrogates' to children in their charge for just a few hours a day." The need for "parent surrogates" arises from "recent trends in family life . . . not necessarily supportive of the development and education of our youth."[23]

It doesn't help when we theorize and complain about *why* kids are lonely today. We know that mothers are working. We know that divorce is epidemic. "I can't worry about why divorces happen," my friend the school counselor told me. "I'm too busy dealing with what is."

"What is" is that kids are alone today and need supportive, nurturing adults more than ever. So if you are a teacher, youth pastor, neighbor, relative, or friend, you may have a tremendous opportunity within your reach. By loving someone else's child, you can keep one more kid from entering troubled waters. You can reach out to a girl drowning in despair. You can provide a solid identity to a teenage boy about to be engulfed by his peers, a rough gang. You can make a difference by loving someone else's child.

Time to get started.

FOUR
Taking the First Step

I spent a year with my uncle Dan and aunt Sue. It was just like I was one of their kids. I went to their church and to school with my cousins, and I made a lot of new friends. I was kind of sorry to go back home because I knew I'd miss everyone, but the break was good for my mom and me. Both of us have our lives more on track now.
—Chrissy, age fifteen

Probably my family's greatest challenge is getting along. My stepdad gets angry easily and doesn't have much patience. He's working on it. He hasn't had any kids of his own, so he probably doesn't really understand everything. That's only from my perspective. The last few nights he's been doing pretty good. He hasn't yelled or gotten angry. My mom and sister went to one of my mom's friend's house, and he and I were by ourselves. It was fun. —Jerry, age twelve

I would tell a stepparent to love their stepchild like your own and realize that we go through many frustrating decisions, and we try to please you and our real parents, so we may get upset and say untrue statements about you. The main thing is just love us and ignore the untrue statements because we thank you for providing for us. —Nikki, age eleven

When you live with a stepparent that cares, it's a real encouragement, 'cause if you had a real parent that doesn't care, it really makes you feel good because someone's there. My stepdad is like my real father, and I love him. —Janice, age fourteen

Give your stepchildren more room to breathe and develop a friendship rather than a "parentship" at first. —Crissy, age sixteen

Are you the type to love someone else's child? Will you make a good step-in parent? In her book *Nobody's Children,* Valerie Bell offers the following characteristics of a nurturing person:

- Nurturers are compassionate. They have the capacity to care and to prove that care through action.
- Nurturers maintain a sense of humor. They can laugh at themselves, and frequently do.
- Nurturers are even-tempered. Nurturers can handle a crisis without making it a catastrophe.
- Nurturers understand children. They do not discipline or dislike children for acting their age.

- Nurturers express affection. They convey to children that they are special by words, attitudes, and significant touches.
- Nurturers are noncompetitive. They can enjoy the superior characteristics of another child without feeling their own children are inferior.
- Nurturers practice an open life-style. There are no dark secrets hidden from view.
- Nurturers maintain a sense of wonder and awe toward life. They enjoy exposing children to God's world.
- Nurturers are trustworthy. They don't gossip about other people's children.
- Nurturers value life and believe in God. They understand they are cooperating in a holy venture when reaching out to a hurting child. They believe they are strategically placed by God and minister his love unreservedly to those with whom they come into contact.[1]

DEFINE YOUR GOAL

It's hard to measure up to those qualifications, isn't it? How can you be all those things? We can't be perfect nurturers, but we can set goals for ourselves and learn how to be the best step-in parents we can be.

How do you love someone else's child? Much will depend on your definition of love. If love to you is a feeling, you will find that you can't automatically love someone else's child in the same way you love your own children or your spouse. But if you define love as a commitment, love can be established on the first day you make a decision to love.

In their study of strong families, Nick Stinnett and John DeFrain list commitment as crucial to any family's success. They define commitment as "an investment of time, energy, spirit, and heart. The family comes first. Family members are dedicated to promoting each other's welfare and happiness—and they expect the family to endure."[2]

Rita Van Tassell, a social worker, says that every step-in family is different, "but our primary goals are the same for all of them: the creation of a loving and secure couple-bond and of a caring space for children to relate both to their natural parents and step[-in] parents."[3]

Whether you commit to loving someone else's child permanently or temporarily depends upon your individual situation. For now, can you agree to commit yourself to love this child or children for *as long as God keeps you together?*

Susan Schultze, with four children, married a man with four children of his own. She first felt insecure in her new role as a step-in mother because the children's biological mother was glamorous and wealthy. But through time, she says, she and her husband and all eight children "grew in depth, and we all learned what real commitment is. We spent several months before we were married in joint outings and get-togethers to see if it was possible for the children to like each other enough to live together. You have to be committed to what is right for each one. It isn't easy, but *don't give up!*"

PRACTICE POSITIVE REGARD

After you've decided to act as a step-in parent for a foster child, a stepchild, a relative, or a grandchild, you need to give the child positive regard. We tend to think that we must accept children unconditionally, as they are, but to be truthful, some aspects of a wounded child may not be acceptable. Perhaps the child is engaging in self-destructive behavior. Perhaps his language or his habits would harm other children in the family. You should not accept these things but still let the child know you will give him positive regard. No matter what he does or says, you will still care for him as a person.

It may not happen immediately, but the child should give you this same positive regard. He may not love you, he may not even want you around, but he should still respect you and your role in his life. In time, he will accept you, but acceptance cannot be forced. You cannot instantly adjust; you must get to know each other on a new level. If you are assuming a new, larger role in the child's life, he must become accustomed to seeing you in that different role.

If you are a step-in parent, don't expect to be automatically called "Mom" or "Dad." These words are more like job descriptions than names, and when a child feels comfortable with you in that role, she'll call you by that name. Until then, though, she may feel more comfortable calling you by your first name or whatever she has called you previously.

Acceptance requires an investment of time. The more time you spend with a child, the more easily she will accept you. Don't concentrate on quality time alone; the *quantity* of time is crucial, too.

The child you want to love may also need to be accepted by other family members. Grandparents should accept the new child and call him or her "my grandchild," just like the biological grandchildren. Foster children should be received and treated on an equal basis with the other children for as long as they are part of the family.

INITIAL CONSIDERATIONS

In her book *Stepmothering: Another Kind of Love,* Pearl Ketover Prilik lists several considerations for prospective stepmothers. I've adapted her list for prospective step-in parents. You and your spouse should discuss the following questions:

- Can our present house handle new family members?
- Do both of us plan to work outside the home?
- Will there be enough time and money for fun?
- How will we share family responsibilities?
- Can we keep our marriage strong through the trials of step-in parenthood?
- What will the children call us?
- Will we have support outside the family?
- What about the kids? How old are they? Who will have legal custody? Why don't the biological parents have custody?
- Are there any special problems we should think about?

- What have the children been told about this future relationship? How will they react to change? To surprises?[4]

ADJUST YOUR EXPECTATIONS

David Lambert teaches a class on parenting in nontraditional families at Kentwood Community Church in Kentwood, Michigan. He has found that most problems in families with step-in parents arise from unrealistic expectations. "Most couples fail to realize that theirs will not be a reconstituted family," he says. "Many times a man or woman will get married and think the new spouse will be the perfect parent for their child, but he or she will never be a substitute for the child's biological parent. The child won't let them fill that role, and they are physically not capable of taking the biological parent's place."

"A lot of families are depressed and in despair at the end of the first year of marriage because they haven't bonded, but stepfamilies aren't brought together quickly. They have to be patient. It takes up to seven years for some stepfamilies to come together."

When Pearl Ketover Prilik married a man with children, she fully expected that her natural maternal instincts would carry over into her stepfamily:

> I quickly discovered that this new kind of mothering, mothering without the touching, the giggling, the luscious intimacy of biological motherhood, was not as natural and easy as I had imagined it would be. My confidence thinned—but my resolve quickened. Constant talking, family

conferences, letter-writing to my husband, my stepchildren, and my son, and the keeping of a personal journal, helped me over the rough spots.

I expected the same kind of love. I found a different kind. I find that I am often a "better" parent toward my stepchildren than I am toward my own son—a more logical, compassionate, calmer parent. There is something noninflammatory in my relationship with my stepchildren; the heat that often fires the bond with my son burns more sedately with my stepchildren.[5]

One stepfather from New York thought that in his second marriage he was sure to be successful—he had learned enough to avoid the mistakes of his first marriage. To build relationships with his new stepchildren, he took a week off work. "Let's go camping this weekend, let's go to a movie, let's play Monopoly, I tell them," he recounts. "But all I get in return are these 'drop dead' looks, and they go running off to their father's house and tell him I pick my teeth after dinner or that my own kids who visit us on weekends are dorks."[6]

Franklin Potter had already raised four children when he married Lorna, who was raising two small children. "I wasn't going to parent them," he says, shrugging. "But I just took over and became the father image. Today I look at them as my children. I was a better father with these two kids than I was with my four."

What can you expect when you first commit yourself to love someone else's child? You should expect confusion, uneasiness, wariness, and neediness. Plan to work hard; to be tested; to feel left out; to become child-centered; to deal with the child's mother, on or off the scene; to feel resistance from the children; to make big efforts; to feel jealous, resentful, and anxious.[7] You might expect to dislike the child you have committed to love. You should expect this experience of commitment to be at least somewhat different from that of raising a biological child. You also should expect that being a step-in parent is, in many ways, fundamentally the same as being a biological parent.

You may go into this relationship clinging to myths. Pearl Prilik lists several false expectations of those who act as step-in parents:

- I'll have "nice" stepchildren.
- Only "real" mothers/fathers have power.
- I'll rescue my husband/wife and his/her children.
- I'll be their real mother/father.
- I'll be a better mother/father than their own.
- This new family will replace their original family.
- They have to love me.
- Love will conquer all.
- This marriage has nothing to do with the kids; they're his/hers.[8]

Perhaps you expect the new children to be just like your biological kids. Or maybe you think that they'll naturally volunteer to help around the house, or that all the kids will get along without squabbling. As Dolly Levi remarks in *Hello, Dolly!* "Whatever you do, for heaven's sake, keep dreaming!"

Why shouldn't there be confusion? Why should your spouse automatically know what's bothering you? Why shouldn't you resent your spouse for disciplining your biological children? Why shouldn't it bother you (or delight you!) when a child's temporary stay has ended? You might be surprised at some of your "unspiritual" reactions after you've agreed to become a step-in parent, but you are human, with natural loyalties and desires. Despite your golden intentions, there will be days when the old flesh cries out and you act or react wrongly. Slow down. Retreat. Pray. Begin again with an apology, and go on.

FOSTER EXPECTATIONS

Marilee Kastle and her husband are raising their ten-year-old daughter and two foster children, ages four and five. "We became foster parents because we wanted to give as many children as we could a stable environment for a period of time," says Marilee. "We want to teach Christian values and practical living skills."

The Kastles have fostered children who returned to the biological mother and thrived. The children with them now, however, have been in the family for three years. "We are disappointed in the system for not speeding up the process of adoption for our current foster children," Marilee told me. "We've tried to provide an example of how a normal family interacts and lives together. All the children are expected to share both the work and the fun. Our relationship with our foster children is different from that with our biological child because it is still a temporary arrangement, and they are aware they will be leaving us someday. It is quite hard to push tender feelings for the two foster children away—they just happen."

In foster care, you might not expect to love the children deeply, but love is sometimes inevitable. "The younger the children are," says Marilee, "the harder it is to turn off any emotional ties to them." And the stronger the emotional ties, the harder the eventual separation will be. Wise foster parents should expect this.

FIND SUPPORT IN THE CHURCH

Many churches are helping nontraditional families learn to live and love God's way, according to his principles. One of the most obvious and helpful tools for families is instruction, and you should look for a church that offers more than a traditional curriculum. Some churches are taking great strides in meeting the needs of changing families, and I hope there is such a church in your area. If there isn't, talk to your church leaders and see if your church can implement one or more of the following programs.

Look for a church that instructs families about healthy relationships. Church leaders should teach what makes a marriage healthy and how to rear children. There are many excellent resources on marriage and family life available, and these books and films could be studied in small discussion groups.

For example, the Parent Education Office of the Roman Catholic Archdiocese of New York has put together a series of courses called "Bringing Families Together."

Look for a church that supports nontraditional families. At Beaverton Christian Church in Beaverton, Oregon, single-parent "teachers" go to single-parent homes to give lessons in parenting. Mel and Phyllis Atkins of Clayton, Missouri, founded a chapter of Grandparents Raising Grandchildren, which meets monthly at their church, St. Marks Evangelical Lutheran Church in University City. At Prestonwood Baptist Church in Richardson, Texas, stepfamilies have their own Sunday school class to handle the sometimes peculiar problems of stepparenting.

Look for a church with established support groups. My church is developing support groups in a number of areas: we have a group for women with hormone imbalances and a group for their husbands; a group for substance abusers and a group for their children or spouses; a group for overeaters; and a group for those who care for elderly parents.

Support groups encourage participants by helping them realize they are not alone in their problems. Practical solutions to common problems are offered, too. I've even heard of a support group whose members take in one another's kids when things get rough at home.

At the New Hope Community Church in Portland, Oregon, a group called Positive Action for Kids convenes while their parents attend a support group. Church leaders realized that if the adults were hurting, so were the kids. In their meeting, the kids give prayer requests and pray with dedicated leaders.

Susan Schultz can remember what it was like to raise children (four) and stepchildren (four) *before* churches helped with innovative programs. "In the early days there wasn't much church support," she says. "We were living through all this before the books and support groups were formed. We had to rely on God and our commitment to one another to do the best we could. That's why I'm really impressed with how churches are committing to help people out in this area.

"As a step-in parent, you will be challenged and tested time and time again, but you have to love the children enough and be a friend so they can learn they can trust you and eventually return that love."

Look for a church that stresses "family night" at home. Frankly, I'd consider it a blessing if the church would call one night "off limits" to any church-sponsored activities. As it is, one of my family could be—and often is—at the church every night of the week. Why not designate Monday night or Thursday night as "family night" and encourage people to stay home and enjoy being together?

"Churches shouldn't program so heavily," said Walt Mueller of Head First Ministries. "And what is programmed should be for the family as a whole. Families need to learn together and play together. If family members are uncomfortable being together, fun activities can help them start interacting."

Look for a church that can offer a network of caring adults to talk to children. When they won't or can't talk to their parents, kids often will open up to another trusted adult, such as a deacon, a youth pastor, a counselor, or a Sunday school teacher. I'll never forget what Gloria Gaither told me once in an interview: "I want my kids to go to people who will tell them what I would have told them had they gone to me," she said. She was talking about her family's extended network of aunts and uncles, but if you don't have that in your town, you can have the church family to support your kids. So encourage friendships between your children and other adults in the church. Don't be threatened or jealous, but rejoice that another adult cares enough to spend time and energy on your children.

Stephanie Archer, who is raising two granddaughters and a stepdaughter, says she would not have made it without spiritual support from others at her church. "I never would have achieved what I have done without my church family. My family didn't support me, but the church has been my family and helped me raise my granddaughters."

LEARN TO LOVE

How do you love someone else's child? Make a commitment to nurture this child for the time you have together; then follow these steps:

Decide to become the child's friend whether or not she immediately responds. Love, after all, is the process of focusing on someone and deciding to make that someone precious to you. Treat her like gold, like a rare treasure. Value her. Give her esteem. The feeling will come later.

Make a conscious effort to become interested in at least one thing that really interests the child. Is it sports? Animals? Clothes? Music? You don't have to become a fanatic, but listen when she talks about her favorite groups and make an effort to keep your eyes from glazing over. Does he adore football? Let him talk about it, and encourage him to get involved. But respect his individuality and don't try to horn in unnecessarily.

Recognize that you and the child are different. Even if you're related, you are different. She is not going to be totally like you. I've often heard adoptive parents and stepparents say with relief, "Well, at least we look alike," as if the lack of a biological link is a dark secret. Being different is nothing to be ashamed of.

So don't be bewildered when your stepdaughter wants to spend all day on the beach and you absolutely hate the sun. We all have different temperaments, personalities, abilities, and tastes. Celebrate the difference!

Learn how to listen. Put everything down, look your child in the eye, and concentrate on what he is saying. Most parents complain that their teenage children never talk to them, but perhaps the kids feel they won't be heard. If a child does talk, celebrate those times. You could say, "I'm glad you told me that. You don't realize how great it is to know what you're thinking and feeling." Be positive. Don't nag and say, "I wish you would . . ." Instead say, "I'm so glad you do . . ." A parent who knows how to show love and appreciation will go far in keeping the doors of communication open. But remember, do all things in moderation. Over-praise may kill a kid's efforts to reach out to you. One woman told me, "Twenty years ago, my mother-in-law got so excited when I called her Mom that I've never been able to bring myself to do it since!"

If your child won't talk, try this approach. Say, "Let me share something with you," and then mention something you've read or thought about. If the child doesn't respond, follow up with, "Have you ever thought about that?" If the child does respond with more than a yes or no, don't argue, even if you disagree. No one wants to be constantly evaluated.

Be willing to invest your time and effort in the relationship. Be more than an "innkeeper." There is more to step-in parenting than cooking and cleaning for a child. Remember, too, to keep your career, your ministry, your personal life, and your family life in perspective.

Give honest praise, comfort, and encouragement when they are due. When the child is hurt, be there to care even if you don't know what to say.

Nothing thrills more than hearing "well done" from an honest critic. When your child asks for your opinion or constructive criticism, give it honestly and gently while emphasizing the positive. Never point out what is wrong without finding two things that are *right.* Help your child to grow better, stronger, and more confident.

Treat your child as a person, not as a baby, a slave, a stranger, or an obligation. See her as her friends see her. Try to see her as God sees her.

Learn to give in gracefully on matters that do not violate spiritual principles. You don't have to win every disagreement. If a child wants to do something and your first inclination is to say no, stop and think—is this something I'm really against, or am I simply refusing because it's more convenient?

Love your spouse unconditionally. Keep your marriage strong and provide a united front as you seek to love this child that God has brought into your life.

Realize that your relationship with this child will be different from other relationships. Do not expect that he or she will naturally feel just like a biological son or daughter. And remember that your commitment to love is not a one-time thing. It is like milk—you have to keep it fresh or it will sour. Your role as a step-in parent will require a daily recommitment to love.

EVALUATE THE DEPTH OF YOUR COMMITMENT

In *Christian Family* magazine, Kathy Bench listed several "think tank" questions for blended families. I have adapted them for step-in families, and I suggest you and your spouse carefully consider them:

- Can you freely tell this child that you respect him?
- Can you bend where traditions clash, or do you insist on your own version of family traditions?
- Are you willing to give the child some undivided attention each day?
- Are you willing to plan activities for you and the child alone?
- In what ways can you show acceptance to this child?
- Does your family pray together regularly?

- Will you expect a different level of performance from this child than from your biological children?
- Will you be tempted to spend money rather than time on this child, hoping to buy his or her acceptance?
- Be honest: can you give this child positive regard and commit to love him for the time God allows you to be together?[9]

FIVE
Adjustments, Big and Small

Don't be afraid to show love for your stepchild.
Don't be closed-minded; be willing to express
your feelings and allow him or her to express
their own feelings! —Pattie, age seventeen

ADJUSTMENTS IN ALL AREAS

Whenever there are changes in a family, the adjustments come in many sizes. A family united through
marriage will face a move and the consequent decisions: your house or mine or a new one? Your dishes
or mine? Do the kids share rooms? Your kids with your
kids or your kids with mine?

Your family will face adjustments about bedtime,
what shows to watch on television, what music to
listen to on the radio, and how to clean the kitchen.
The older the children are, the more they will have set
ideas about how things should be.

Families stepping in as foster homes face adjustments, too. Who gives up his personal space? Who

will be responsible for taking the child for visits with a biological parent or siblings? What if the foster child wants to watch "Sesame Street" and your kids are adamant about watching "Star Trek" at the same time?

Sometimes step-in parents are so busy adjusting themselves that they forget about the adjustments the children have had forced upon them. The child in your care must adjust to many losses, including old friends, a parent, and dreams and expectations about his or her original family. So don't allow yourself to feel like a martyr—you, your family, and your new child are all making adjustments to be together.

FOOD

One of the most sensitive and quickly revealed areas of adjustment is food. Bill and Janet Wright married and shared six children between them. "Bill's kids turned up their noses at my cooking," Janet recalls. "I had been on a strict budget, and I always cooked huge, inexpensive casseroles. After working all day for a family with six kids, I wasn't too thrilled with their attitudes."

Mick Leeward found that mealtimes were difficult because his stepson was a picky eater. Mick felt as if he was constantly urging the child to eat, so the kitchen table became a battlefield three times a day.

STRUCTURE

The child who enters your home probably will have to adjust to a different family structure. Families come in two basic styles, structured and unstructured, with a thousand variations in between. Structured families eat at certain established times (with no snacks in between, unless it's at a predetermined snack time), and bedtime is strictly observed. They thrive on bedtime rituals: a bath, prayers, a story, and a kiss on the head. The parents then enjoy the quiet hours of privacy when the children are in bed.

Unstructured families come and go as they please. They let the kids stay up until they fall asleep on the floor, and the kids are allowed to snack whenever they're hungry. Parents in unstructured families enjoy having their kids around, going out at midnight for impulsive fun, and generally being flexible.

"When a child from one style of family goes into a family with a different style, it's a big adjustment," says Linda Post, a guidance counselor who works with middle school kids. "It's a constant, everyday struggle because it involves daily rituals. These exact routines were established before the child's new family was."

Post prefers the structured style for parenting because, without it, "there is no expected free time for the adults." It's hard to be a parent, and it's even harder when you can't look forward to an hour or two of relief.

LOSS OF CONTROL

When a child arrives in your home, be prepared to sacrifice a great deal of control over your time, privacy, and possessions. Marilee Kastle, who is stepping in as a foster mother for a boy and girl who arrived at ages three years and sixteen months, says the adjustment was difficult because of the age difference between the foster children and her biological daughter who was eight when the new children arrived. "We were thrown back into a baby stage—with playpens, high chairs, and cribs—that we thought we had outgrown. We couldn't pick up and go at a moment's notice any longer. The boy wet the bed every night for six months and had to be kept off the furniture because he drooled on everything and did not speak.

"Food was one of the only things that was *not* a problem. They ate anything and everything we gave them because their biological parents had fed them junk food every day. The baby had nightmares every night, but came around much better initially than the boy did. It was frustrating to work with them, though, because they did not have the quick mind and response rate of our daughter."

Steve Newton laughs at the memory of the early days when he married Elaine and became a father to her sons, ages twelve and fourteen. "When I first married, almost everything in the house was from my previous apartment, it was all mine. Over the first year, the things I was in control of shrank. Now I can only consider the top of my desk in the bedroom mine. I wanted everything that was mine to be used only the way I wanted it to be used, and I had to give up control of the furniture, my tools, everything. I had to realize I couldn't tell them how to use what used to be mine, because now it was ours."

Another step-in father reported, "Kids tend to take over whatever is there. That was hard. During all my years on my own I had sort of developed a system. You know, you put something here, and that's where it always is: stamps live here, the flashlight lives there, that sort of thing. All of a sudden the stamps were never there, the flashlight was never there. You'd always have to hunt for them. Those kinds of things could be very annoying."[1]

Steve Newton agrees, but adds: "It's been worth it. My prayers were answered when I met Elaine. I had been suicidal before, I was so lonely, and I cried out to God because I didn't want to live anymore. When I quit looking, God brought Elaine into my life, and I found out she had children. There were only a few days where I was fearful if this was the right situation for me.

"But now I know the boys are the answer to my prayers. There's never a lonely moment around here."

SHARE THE FUN, SHARE THE WORK

Children judge whether or not they are accepted as a part of the family by our actions, not our words. The day Amanda Morgan married her second husband "was an exhilarating day for me," she writes, "but my wedding was an entirely different experience for Jenny."

Jenny, Amanda's daughter from her first marriage, told her mother the wedding day was the worst day of her life: "Even though I really liked Harry, I was used to being The One, you know? And then the party was centered around you and him, and people said, 'Here's to the husband and wife.' Well, what about the daughter? When it was time to cut the cake, no one even noticed that I was in the room. You guys fed each other, but nobody fed me."[2]

When families come together, it is important to recognize each family member and his or her place in the family. Being part of a family is sharing not only in the love and the fun, but also in the responsibilities. No one wants to be Cinderella, the stepdaughter who had all work and no play, but it is good for kids to share in family chores.

"Divorced moms tend to make up for their guilt about their divorce and remarriage by going easy on the children, with the result that the kids don't do a thing around the house," writes Amanda Morgan. "So who ends up doing the work? Most often, it's Mom, who, resentful of her unfair share of the work burden, ends up taking her frustrations out on the kids and her husband."[3]

Not only do moms need a break, but kids need to feel that they are part of a functioning household. There is no better way to feel a part of something than to be partly responsible for its care and upkeep. The old axioms are true: you appreciate something more when you've worked for it, and if you have to clean up a mess, you'll think twice about making it.

Happy families share the chores and support one another. "From the time we were married, we pitched in and helped each other," one wife told Dolores Curran, author of *Stress and the Healthy Family*. "Whether it was with housework or outside work. Our kids just followed that example as they grew up."[4]

To ensure that everyone does his or her fair share,

sit down with your family and list all household chores. Then divide them evenly and according to the ability of each child.

I use the "tickle file" system to clean my house. I list each household chore on a notecard and keep it in a recipe box. At the top of each card is the name of the chore, and in the left-hand corner I write how often the chore should be done: once a week, daily, or monthly, for instance. In the right-hand corner I indicate which kids are capable of completing that chore.

Every morning when we get up, I simply pull out the cards behind the day's date, and my family and I complete those chores. When we're done, we refile the cards according to when the chores are due to be done again.

It may sound crazy, but the system works. We're spared from compulsive cleaning (if it's dirty, we know it will be cleaned eventually), but important chores are done first thing every morning, and they don't hang over our heads all day. When everyone helps clean up and work around the house, it becomes a home, not a hotel.

TAKE TIME FOR THE FAMILY

When children "step in" to your home, you may have to adjust the amount of time you spend with your family. Healthy, committed families make family a priority. When I was engaged to my husband, a youth pastor, I heard one of my Christian professors remark that he didn't want his five children to attend all the church youth activities. I was stunned. Not go to church every time something was offered?

"If I sent my kids to church every time there was a youth activity," he explained, "I'd never see them. At our church, there's something practically every night." After thinking about it, I realized what he said was true.

Today, when women and men work outside the home and kids are involved in school, sports, gymnastics, part-time jobs, and neighborhood organizations, it's a rare family that finds itself intact on any given night of the week. But successful, committed families block out time for themselves.

Dr. Stephen A. Timm, a clinical psychologist, stresses the need to set aside time in advance for family recreation. "Get your calendar and plan activities and time together for the entire year," he advises. "Make these times sacred and untouchable. There is a minimum amount of time that families must spend together to maintain harmony and well-being. That amount varies from family to family, but when a family drops below its minimum, problems appear."[5]

If planning a yearly calendar seems impossible, try setting aside one night a week as a sacred "family night." Allow nothing to interrupt your family time, and allow a different family member each week to plan the night's activity. Dean and Grace Merrill have written a terrific book, *Together at Home* (Thomas Nelson Publishers), with fifty-two ideas for weekly family nights through the year.

With a strong family identity, the child you are seeking to love will begin to feel that she is part of something larger than her own struggles, losses, and fears. She will be part of a family, and a strong family can survive.

KEEP YOUR MARRIAGE STRONG

Whether you are committing yourself to loving a step-child, a foster child, a grandchild, or some other child, you must make sure to keep your marriage strong. Initially in a stepfamily, it may be difficult for husbands and wives to solidify their relationship: it is overshadowed by the strong bond that already exists between the mother or father and the biological children. The new spouse may feel that he or she is intruding on an already established relationship. But the bond between the husband and wife must be strong if the family is to pull—and stay—together.

Emily Visher, a therapist in Palo Alto, California, says "It's hard to have a honeymoon in the middle of a crowd, but you really need to nourish the couple relationship."[6] She suggests that couples buy an inexpensive "Do Not Disturb" sign and post it next to the *locked* bedroom door. Passion should be saved for the bedroom, but parents shouldn't be afraid to show affection in front of the kids. They need to know that the marriage is strong, and affection is a part of that.

Mary F. Whiteside, a psychologist affiliated with the Ann Arbor, Michigan, Center for the Family, identifies "the need to establish a firm marital coalition" as an important task of early remarriage. "If the couple fails," explains a husband who recently celebrated the tenth anniversary of marriage to his second wife, "then so will the stepfamily."[7]

Helayne Malamood, who runs a Families-in-Step program, says, "The only way a second marriage can work is if there is ample time geared toward being a couple. A couple has to work hard at developing a relationship and not falling into the trap of focusing all their energies on the kids. Unless you're solid as a couple, you can never create a family identity. And that means you have to spend time alone with each other, doing a lot of talking."[8]

Couples must act as a united coalition, especially when dealing with children from a previous marriage. If a father makes decisions concerning his children and those decisions affect his wife, she should be consulted.

David Lambert, who teaches a class for parents of nontraditional families at Kentwood Community Church, says remarried couples have a hard time when one spouse feels guilty about not spending enough time with his or her biological child. If a biological parent feels that he is shortchanging his child, he may spend a lot of time at Little League games, PTA meetings, and shopping for kids' clothes, and very little time with his new spouse. The new spouse feels left out, and as a result, the marriage is severely weakened.

"A marriage cannot be healthy when the adult-child bond is stronger than the bond between the two adults," Lambert says. "The problem usually is that the husband and wife spend too little time together. They rarely go out on dates, and they're more into their job or the kids than into their marriage relationship."

Even in the case of foster parents or grandparents, who are not dealing with a second marriage, the marriage must remain strong. The stresses of child rearing, multiplied by the fact that this is someone else's

child, can take the focus off the marital relationship
and put it on the child or children. Couples who want
to reinforce their positions as leaders of the home
must make time to be together.

In today's rushed and harried world, it is not always
easy to make time. Be imaginative. Meet for lunch
once a week. Call each other during the day just to
"check in." Turn down invitations so you can be
together. Leave notes around the house. My husband
often writes messages to me in soap on the bathroom
mirror—he knows once I'm awake in the morning, I'll
see the "I love you" he scrawled over the sink.

Couples who want to remain strong also should do
something together, such as studying the Bible or
team-teaching a Sunday school class. Jog together.
Play tennis. Sing duets. Develop something that is not
job-related that you can enjoy with each other.

Don't forget, though, that even the most extroverted
person needs some time alone. My father likes to
tramp through the woods or tinker in his garage workshop. My mother likes to read. I like to work in my
office. My husband likes to stand in the driveway and
endlessly shoot a basketball through a hoop. All of us
have pursuits that we enjoy doing alone. This need
to be alone does not diminish when a child joins the
family. It may increase. Provide for it.

HOLIDAY TRADITIONS

Perhaps one of the most volatile areas of adjustment
is holiday traditions. How can you allow a child to
spend time at Christmas with everyone who is

important to him? What do you do with holiday traditions from a family that is no longer intact? Insist upon them? Discard them? Reinvent them? Combine them with traditions from new family members? And how do you get everyone together for the holiday when other people have ties to your children?

"The holiday demands that families be together," said one divorced father who has now remarried. "If I don't have the kids, I ache. If I do have the kids, returning them to their mother after Christmas can be just as devastating. In fact, the mere anticipation of having to return them after the holiday can put a damper on the whole holiday if I don't stay on guard against the feelings."[9]

Families with recently arrived children can face special problems. During Mary Sutter's first Christmas with stepchildren, a teenage daughter refused to participate and never even got dressed. And despite Mary's best efforts to give all eleven children gifts of equal value, her biological son accused her of spending more on her stepchildren than on her own. "I was devastated," Mary says. "That first holiday was a complete period of disillusionment."[10]

Part of the problem is that we raise our holiday expectations too high and are unwilling to compromise. "I know some families who refuse to have Christmas dinner on any day but the twenty-fifth," one mother told me. "But with our children, we choose an alternate day. I don't care—I'd have it on December first if that is when everybody could get together."

We expect our holidays to be of the Ozzie and Harriet variety with everyone gathered around the dining room table, but that is a dangerous expectation. "The pressure to conform to this illusion can create serious family tensions," says Patricia Stevens, a psychologist in Brooklyn. "In fact, the perfect family, congenial and relaxed together, involved in a mutual effort toward common goals, may not be the reality at all. It may not be financially feasible for everyone to gather several generations of the family in one place for the big meal. The result can be feelings of anger, even rage, because one's family falls short of the impossible ideal."[11]

The Hermanns, a California family, have learned how to enjoy Christmas with their children *as they pass through the house*. In early December, they buy a large tree and begin decorating it, knowing that it won't be complete until everyone has had a chance to help. The family exchanges gifts throughout the holiday season, and cookie baking is a recurrent activity with the children. "We always have scattered activities throughout the season," says Kathleen Hermann. "The presence of each other is the main thing we want to enjoy. Instead of trying to have a perfect holiday, we try to have a few really special moments that we really concentrate on."[12]

When it comes to deciding where and with whom the children spend a holiday, Dr. Lee Salk reminds us that kids always need to feel they have some impact on the world, and children of divorce have an even greater need to feel they have an influence on some of the decisions that govern their lives. "At the very least," he says, "it would be a good idea to say, 'Well, we were thinking of your spending Christmas Eve with your mother and Christmas Day with your dad, unless you have some objection?' Don't interpret the child's choice as a rejection, since children carry a residue of guilt for their parents' split as it is. What the youngsters decide may just be more convenient or emotionally easier for them."[13]

Of course, some children will be too young to make a choice, or geographic distance or some other situation will make it impossible for them to spend Christmas at any place other than your house. As you establish holiday traditions at your home, try keeping some old traditions as well as incorporating new ones.

One foster mother told me that her foster son arrived with no traditions or expectations about holidays. "One of the biological parents of our foster son told me that Christmas was like any other day. Also, the children in that family were nearly ignored on their birthdays! How does a foster child feel after he has experienced holidays in beautiful ways and then goes back to nothing?"

Perhaps foster parents could teach children private holiday rituals. For instance, on special holidays foster parents could light a candle and tell their foster child, "On this day we'll always light a candle and think of you. On this day you can light one and think of us." It's a small gesture but something that could reassure foster children that loving foster parents are thinking of them.

Psychologist Patricia Papernow realizes that holidays can accentuate the loss a child has experienced. Because of this loss and the subsequent change, she says, "there is a tremendous need to keep the ritual the same."

Children and adults find comfort in the familiar rituals. To keep tensions to a minimum, Papernow suggests that new families discuss which rituals to keep and which to change, reschedule, or discard. She recommends including the children—often their ideas are the most creative. She also suggests choosing a "virgin holiday"— a holiday for which there are no prescribed rituals, and designating that day as a unique family holiday.[14] Perhaps Groundhog Day or Sweetest Day or the first day of summer—any of these could be the holiday that brings your family together and builds lasting memories.

There is no easy answer to the holiday conundrum. You may not be able to make everyone happy. Begin your own traditions, and let your children know that no matter where they are or what they're doing, you are thinking of them on this special holiday. Don't let yourself become upset or depressed if for some reason your child is unable to spend the holiday with you.

Dr. Salk says, "A parent who doesn't get to be with the children on a significant day may feel particularly prone to the holiday blues. One of the best ways to ensure some degree of sanity at this time of year is to make your plans, allowing room for your children to join in, and not leave yourself vulnerable to everybody else's decisions. If you feel you need your children to make the season happy and they have other choices, there are bound to be problems."[15]

More practical advice:

- Don't attempt to compete through presents. It helps if you and the children's biological parent(s) agree about what gifts would be appropriate for the child.

- Don't tell the kids they're lucky to get two (or more!) sets of presents.
- Don't forget grandparents.
- Expect the children to experience some anxiety and guilt. If they are traveling from one household to another, they are likely to be nervous. If they have just a short visit with a biological parent, they are likely to feel guilty for saying, "Have a happy holiday," and then leaving. In fact, the more they enjoy the holiday at your house, the more guilt they may feel about their absent parent(s).
- Invite the child's biological parent(s) to the celebration at your home only if there is a genuinely cooperative spirit. Younger children may have trouble understanding why Mom or Dad is present one day and gone the next.

FINANCES

When your family increases with step-in children, you may have to make certain financial adjustments. Maybe you can't afford to give six kids five dollars' allowance each week. Now that your budget and family have grown, perhaps you expect your kids to earn their own spending money by baby-sitting, mowing lawns, or getting a part-time job. Kids who have been used to a generous free allowance may rebel against the establishment of new standards.

Marguerite Kelly married a man who had three children from a previous marriage, and they've had a baby together. The family has adjusted well. "Money is the only problem," she wrote in the *Washington Post.* "My husband pays $1,000 a month for child support, but the children—especially the girls—complain. They say it isn't enough money for camp and for the clothes they want and sometimes they say he is cheap.

"Children still will want more than they can have," Kelly says. "That's just human nature and it shouldn't cause you a single twinge of guilt. Children aren't supposed to be spoiled."

Kelly suggests helping teenagers see how the money is spent and how far it can be stretched with careful shopping and budgeting. "A sixteen-year-old—even a thirteen-year-old—can work with you," she says, suggesting that kids help balance the checkbook. And if they still complain about a money shortage, "give them sympathy instead of a lecture: 'Of course you want more clothes. We'd love to be able to give them to you.' Love and understanding are the currency that count," says Kelly.[16]

SIX
Defining Roles

The best thing about living with a stepfather is that I get different points of view on my problems. My stepdad is becoming one of my best friends because he listens and acts like a friend and a father. He's the best! —Patricia, age fourteen

One great concern of step-in parents is how to assume a traditional role in a nontraditional situation. Foster parents are Mom and Dad, but only temporarily. Grandparents raising grandchildren are not doting sweeties who supply love and kisses and then send the kids back to Mom and Dad for discipline. Step-parents may not even have a title: the kids won't call you Mom or Dad, and you would feel a little strange if they called you by your first name. So you settle for being "Hey, you" for a while.

In the beginning, you and the kids may not know who and what you are supposed to be. But outside your family, other people will be quick to voice their opinions about the role you are undertaking:

"You're a foster parent? Oh, I could never do that. I hear the money's pretty good though, huh?"

"You're really the grandparents? Are you crazy? At your age, you shouldn't be raising kids!"

"So you're a wicked stepmother. Boy, his wife must have really been a witch if the kids are living with you."

"Only a stepfather? Boy, are you a sap. How'd you get saddled with a wife and some other guy's kids?"

"You adopted these kids? Don't you worry about them running off to find their *real* parents?"

TIME OUT FOR STEPPARENTS

Before we go any further in the exploration of appropriate roles in the family, let's just take a moment to acknowledge that while step-in parents have many things in common, there are also several major differences among them.

Biological parents bond with their children and nurture them with the full acceptance of society. Grandparents share a similar bond. Part-time stepparents limit their involvement with the children: for a weekend or a week or a month in the summer, they are friends and buddies, but their time and emotional involvement is limited. Adoptive parents choose to accept full responsibility for their children, but bonds are broken or never established with the biological parents (except in open adoption, but that contact is usually limited). Foster parents recognize from the start that the relationship is temporary.[1]

Different from all the others, stepparents who have custody of the stepchildren often feel that they live in limbo, not allowed to fully parent the children, and not able to separate emotionally from them, either. Step-parents are not baby-sitters or substitutes or part-time help. Perhaps theirs is the most difficult role to define and fill successfully.

STEP-IN PARENTS WEAR MANY HATS

As you undertake to love someone else's child, you may find that you know little or nothing about raising children. Child rearing requires that you be part nurse, economist, dietitian, chauffeur, psychologist, diplomat, and teacher. Can you fill those roles?

What does it mean when a kid has a fever but no rash? Can Johnny really be healthy if he only eats pizza and bananas? Why is thirteen-year-old Mary moping around in her room with the door closed? Is it normal for a six-year-old boy to scream at the top of his lungs all day? Do five-year-olds go to slumber par-ties? If Marcie has a question about sex, do you send her to her biological mother? To her father? Do you handle it? Does she trust you? Do you trust yourself?

If you buy Tommy a big, fancy cake for his birthday, will he think you're trying to "show up" his biological mother or father? Will your biological children feel threatened or resentful if you do for Tommy what you did for them?

What happens if you or your spouse dies? Will the children stay with the surviving spouse? Will they go elsewhere? Is there someone you can trust and talk to when things aren't going well?

You will grow confident in your parenting abilities

as time passes. All parents, biological or otherwise, make mistakes and learn from them. None of us is infallible, none of us knew all the answers before we began to raise children. In fact, none of us will know all the answers even after the children are grown and gone and reasonably successful! So whatever your role becomes, do your best before God and your family, and you can be confident as a step-in mother or father to the child in your life.

It is important that you understand your role and grow confident in it. Researchers who studied strong families found three characteristics in successful families: strong families are committed to one another; strong families share a religious or spiritual orientation; and strong families are guided by clear role definitions so that each member knows his or her duties in the face of crises and problems.[2]

Steve Newton wondered what his role would be in the lives of his wife Elaine's two teenage sons. "At my wedding, though, my best man gave me this piece of advice: anyone can come along and be their friend, but you're the only one that can be the father in the home. So as much as these children will let you be, realize your responsibility and be a father to these boys.

"I decided to consider them my boys right from the beginning. I wanted our relationship to be intimate and close, and I wanted them to come to me with their problems and ask for permission, but that had to grow over time. At first, it was just a matter of trusting me. They wanted to be sure I wouldn't leave their mom, and it took six months before they really believed our marriage would be long-term.

"Plus, my sons are two different people. The younger boy always wanted a father, but he thought fathers were always nice, friendly, and helpful. He was rebellious at first when I asked him to do things, but I was able to work things out with him quickly because he is verbal and challenges things openly. My older son is quiet and stays to himself, and it is just in the last year, after three years of marriage, that he has realized I am his father and I can tell him to do things. I've earned his respect and the love has grown. I feel comfortable giving him a hug now, but I'm less physical with the boys than their mother is. When we do hug, it tends to be when we're working out a problem or when they've done something really great."

DANGEROUS ROLES

As a step-in parent, you may be tempted to assume an inappropriate role in the family. For instance, you should not be merely the *housekeeper* or *breadwinner*. You will never be considered part of the family if you limit yourself to a role that could be easily filled by hired help. Don't allow yourself to be simply a *husband* or *wife* either. You are a companion for more than one person. Finally, don't assume you can be satisfied simply by being a *friend* to the new child.

If you live in the home, you must find a role in the family. Constance Ahrons, a professor of sociology at the University of Southern California, found that step-in mothers frequently struggle with inappropriate roles. Given that men usually marry younger women, the small age difference between women and their stepchildren may incline step-in mothers to feel they should be more a peer or a friend than a mother-figure.[3]

But if you are a step-in parent, you are more than a friend to this child.

Friends don't instruct; step-in parents do.

Friends have shared interests; step-in parents and their children may not.

Friends enjoy each other's company; step-in parents and their children may not.

Friends don't live together; step-in parents and their children may.

Friendships are fragile; step-in parent and child relationships should be strong.[4]

AGES AND STAGES

In your role as a step-in parent, it is important that you have a good understanding of children and their characteristics at various ages. If you are parenting a young child, you have a tremendous opportunity for a long-term relationship. Children younger than three are most readily integrated into a new family, says family therapist Thomas Seibt. "That's when they haven't had an opportunity to get to know their biological parent that well."[5]

Young children are amazingly resilient, but they are also immature and ill equipped to handle adult problems. You cannot unload your adult emotions or problems on a young child.

If God brings a young child into your life, prepare to be flexible and cautious. Be willing to talk openly about the past. A child may have questions about why his home split up, why he can't be with his mommy or daddy, or who you are. He may have fears voiced only in his play or in his nightmares. When you talk with your child, reassure him that he is not at fault for whatever happened in his home. Because children do not have complete understanding and are usually sheltered from the entire truth, they often feel guilty about the changes in their lives.

Answer your child's questions as completely and honestly as you can. Always tell the truth, but only as much as the child can handle. Don't go into sordid details, but explain that God has brought you into his life for a purpose and for now. Don't promise to be with the child forever if you can't fulfill the promise.

If the child can't verbalize his or her fears, you might try suggesting some questions yourself. Perhaps you could use a doll or the example of a friend. For instance, you might say: "Tommy's parents divorced last year, and now Tommy has a new mommy. Do you think he likes her? Do you think he's afraid she might leave, too?"

Whatever you do, do not criticize the child's biological parents. State the truth: "Your mommy is an alcoholic" or "Your daddy had to go to prison" or "Your mommy wants to live with another man." Do not say "Your mommy is a witch and a terrible person." Or "Your daddy has never loved you kids, he doesn't know how to love anyone."

Children need to feel a kinship with their biological parents. They are part of them. They need to accept that part of themselves without harsh criticism. If they cling to a rosy and inflated image of their absent parent, don't burst the bubble. Time and maturity will reveal the truth.

Remind your child often that God loves her very much. Show your love by spending time with her. Time is the love language of children.

Tell your child every day that you love her, not only in words but by your actions. Dr. Clyde Narramore of the Narramore Christian Foundation told me about giving an IQ test to a little boy. The boy looked up and said, "Know what, Mister? My daddy loves me."

"Are you sure?" Dr. Narramore asked.

"Yep."

"But, Jimmy, how do you know?"

"Because he likes to play with me."

We tell children we love and value them by encouraging them to talk to us. Another way is by not comparing them with the other children in the home. Dr. Narramore says, "Being continually and unfavorably compared with another deeply humiliates a child. He will dislike the one doing the comparing, he will dislike the one he is compared to, and he will also dislike himself."

Finally, lead your child in paths of righteousness. Explain everything in spiritual terms as much as possible. The other morning my six-year-old, Tyler, climbed into bed with me. "I want a morning hug," he said sleepily. I groggily threw my arms around his neck, then murmured, "Did you know God wants to talk to us in the morning, too?"

Tyler perked up. "He does?"

"Morning, noon, and night, that's what the Bible

says," I answered, looking my little boy in the eye. "Praying is like giving God a morning hug three times a day."

You can teach spiritual lessons even when you are just walking outside. You can point to a tree and explain that it is a wonderful creation of God—the roots go down deep into the soil and draw up water and nutrients, and the leaves bring in sunlight and make food for the tree to grow. You can point to the birds and explain how God gifted them for flight. Lessons like these will help your children realize that nothing is an accident, especially not them. They are wonderful, exciting creations of God.

Dr. Narramore says, "Children can understand unconditional love and forgiveness through Christ and can learn to respect God's holy Word, but these truths are best grasped through parents' examples, not through forceful teaching or overemphasized religious discipline. The impressions of God formed by young children can greatly influence their lifelong beliefs."[6]

THE "TWEENAGE" YEARS

Perhaps the hardest ages for children to enter new families are between nine and fifteen.[7] They may have had more responsibilities or privileges in their previous home than they will have in their new home. Plus, they are approaching or going through puberty, when internal changes are hard enough to handle without external pressures, too.

When children are younger, says Mavis Hetherington of the University of Virginia, a warm and loving step-in parent can be accepted rather easily. When seventeen- and eighteen-year-olds have a step-in parent, it relieves them of their concern that their biological parent is going to be lonely when they leave home.

"But kids in the nine-to-fifteen age group are struggling with their own independence, and here comes this outsider interfering. And they are struggling with their own awakening sexuality, and they don't want to think of their [parents] as sexual beings. It's very difficult to recognize that."[8]

My husband and I have a special place in our hearts for "tweens," children between the ages of eleven and fourteen. These kids are between childhood and the more liberated teenage years, and they are unique.

I'll never forget when Linda stopped me in the hall at church. "Can you recommend any good books for me on kids?" she said, looking faintly worried. "My husband's daughter stays with us on weekends, and she's thirteen. I don't have the faintest idea what she's going through or what to talk to her about."

Tweens may seem strange, but those years of sixth, seventh, and eighth grades bring with them a confusing array of conflicting emotions, habits, and friendships. It's hard enough to raise a tween in an intact family—how are you going to love someone else's tween?

First, understand what these kids are going through. Strictly speaking, adolescence begins at puberty, but each child enters adolescence on his or her individual timetable. Puberty itself may occur when a child is as young as nine or as old as eighteen, but the social changes of the teen years begin affecting most children by age eleven. Tempers flare, tears flow, doors slam. Tweens are, in a word, extreme. Consciously pulling away from the world of childhood, tweens push full throttle into what they perceive as an adult world. But they can't venture into that world alone. To feel secure, they must find two things: a hero and a peer group.

Tweens worship their heroes. Whether the hero is a basketball sensation, the hottest rock star, or a cool teacher at school, tweens imitate and idolize him or her. Many parents feel jealous and threatened when they begin to hear their children praising a hero. "I had always thought I was my son's hero," one dad said. "Then one day he came home talking about his coach. I'll admit it, I was jealous. I couldn't believe there was another father figure in his life."

Relax! Tweens are beginning to expand their horizons beyond the home. In fact, most tweens would rather die than be seen in public with their parents. It is not that they don't love or need parents anymore; they are simply embarrassed by the adult/child role that was appropriate in earlier years. A tween is ashamed to be seen having a parent do something for him (buy his clothes, give him a ride to the mall) that he cannot yet do for himself.

Tweens need parents as much as children of any age, possibly even more than most. But tweens need parents as a safety net, not as a front line of defense. If your tween seems to avoid you in public, it is their time to begin meeting the world on their own. So it may not be that your child hates having you as a step-in parent, it's just that she wants to be independent.

Let your child know you are there for him or her. If he or she is embarrassed by your hugs and kisses, refrain from displays of affection in public. Boys are particularly embarrassed when Mom or Dad reaches for a hug or kiss. But in the privacy of the home, parents should continue to show affection even though their tween may not respond. As much as possible, parents should also be available to do things their tween wants to do. Tweens still need to know they are loved.

Tweens are among the most insecure people on earth, and they congregate in groups to gain strength through group conformity. One mother asked why her daughter had to have four holes in each ear. "It's just too different," sighed the mother.

"But Mom, I've got to be different!" the daughter explained. "How else can I be like everybody else?"

Tweens find approval and security within the ranks of their peers. If your tween has established a group of friends, soon you will notice that the group dresses, talks, walks, and thinks alike. Peer pressure will never be stronger than at this age.

Your child's ability to stand up to his friends will depend on which influence is stronger in his life: his friends or his family. In our work with tweens, my husband and I have discovered that kids from families who work to keep a strong and wholesome family identity consistently overcome negative peer group influences. Tweens need to feel they are a part of something—either a strong family or a strong peer group. If the family and the peer group share the same convictions, a child can have both. But if the family lacks a sense of unity, the child will feel more at home among his peers.

How much time does your family spend together? Again, let me stress the importance of setting aside weekly family time. Let nothing interrupt these times of family togetherness, and don't forget to let your tweens have a say in what they think would be fun. Since many tweens are adverse to going out in public with their families, maybe a movie night at home with big bowls of popcorn would be more to their taste.

Don't ever be surprised by what a tween will do. Tweens, particularly boys, are known for their extreme humor and manners. "My son and his friends just sit around all afternoon to see who can belch the loudest," one mother complained. "They're so gross! I know the kid has good manners, but lately they've flown out the window."

Extreme insensitivity to others is another trait of tweens. Tweens can be unbelievably cruel to one another and to step-in parents, verbally attacking with venom rare in children. They may giggle at the handi-capped, ape the mannerisms of senior adults, or call stinging insults to a kid who is overweight. They need to be reminded of thoughtfulness and courtesy.

Perhaps they make fun of others because they feel so awkward themselves. Their bodies are beginning to grow to adult proportions, and their emotions skitter up and down because of the hormonal upheaval. When they were young children, their emotions were dependent upon external circumstances—they were happy because someone gave them something or did something for them. As tweens, however, their emotions spring from what is going on inside, and those emotions vacillate wildly from day to day, hour to hour. Girls are generally two years ahead of the boys in development, and this difference does nothing to encourage self-esteem or confidence for either sex.

Tweens explore this new sense of growth and physical prowess in the privacy of their bedrooms. Boys prance and sing in front of the mirror. Girls practice kissing on their mirrors and dream of romance and love. With harmless daydreaming and imagination come the dark clouds of the tween years—rebellion. Parents usually notice two types of rebellion. The first is not rebellion as much as simple testing. "You're not going to the movies Monday night," you may say, expecting your word to be law.

Your tween will look you in the eye and ask, "Why?"

If you yell, "Because I said so," you have lost the war. You may win the battle, but your tween will only stalk off, convinced that you are unreasonable, stubborn, and just plain mean.

If, however, you take the time to calmly explain— "It's a school night and your mother and I don't want you out late"—your child may not agree, but he will see the reason behind the rule.

Tweens have the difficult task of taking the rules and guidelines they learned as children and testing them according to the standards presented by society. They will test what their parents have taught. If the principles work, fine. If not, tweens are likely to cast them aside. When a child is mature, he will present his parents with a new set of philosophies: his own.

The second type of rebellion results from a broken promise and is common among children from broken homes. The "promise" need not be spoken; in fact, it is often a presumption. "Just be yourself and people will like you," a mother tells her daughter. The daughter tries being herself but feels ugly, insecure, and socially inept. Worse yet, she is not accepted at school.

My mother was wrong, the girl concludes, *so I'm not going to trust her advice anymore.* Consequently, the girl rebels against her mother and anyone else she deems untrustworthy. She hides her hurt and disillusionment behind a wall of indifference.

When tweens give up on adults because of a broken promise, counsel from a wise adult is usually necessary. Tweens often lack the emotional maturity and psychological resources to resolve their disappointment.

To parent tweens wisely and well, it is so important that we *talk* to them. Life today moves at a hectic pace, and the tweenage years are too fleeting. So take your child out to lunch during the school day. Carry a bowl of popcorn into his or her room at bedtime and talk. Listen carefully, with your eyes and your heart as well as your ears. Make time available for your child to reach out to you. Let him or her know that you are always ready to listen.

The tween years can be a bit bizarre, but they are precious. Each day your tween becomes less like a child and more like the adult he or she will become. Take time to share in the wonder of growth. Be there for love and laughter when you can.

TEENAGERS

"Hire a teenager, while he still knows everything," proclaimed the bumper sticker on the car in front of me. I had to laugh—it's true. I knew everything when I was a teenager, or at least I thought I did. The world was in front of me, I could drive, and I wanted my independence!

Choosing to love someone else's teenager is far more difficult than loving someone else's tiny baby. Teenagers are already formed, they are independent, and they are aloof. They are not always warm and fuzzy. "Teens come with so much 'baggage'" exclaimed one foster mother.

Young children accept help and discipline from a new parental figure much more quickly than does a teenager. Young children still depend physically and emotionally on parental figures; teenagers do not. Instead, teenagers are preoccupied with their changing sexuality, schoolwork, friends, sports, and their quest for independence. They don't want to spend time with their biological parents, much less with a stepparent, foster parent, or guardian.

Jon Nordheimer tells of a New Jersey businessman who married a woman with teenagers. The stepfather told his stepson he should not watch an R-rated cable movie. "My dad lets me watch 'em," the kid replied. "And besides, it's Mom's television set."

"I don't know how I made it through that first year without killing that kid," the man said.

"In the beginning of a remarriage, stepdads should be like polite strangers in their new wife's home and talk to the teenage kids, but not intervene or exercise too much control over their lives," says Mavis Hetherington. "There's too much hostility in the kids who at that age want independence, not control."[9]

Teenagers find it harder than younger children to accept new rules. A fifteen-year-old boy who divides his time between two homes says, "When I lived with both my parents, things were pretty casual. If I got in late some Saturday night, they'd remark on it, but it was no big deal, like it is here. If I brought home a note saying I'd missed class, my father would be disappointed and later that night he'd talk to me about it. Here, if that happens, my stepmother gets mad and yells. When I came here first, she'd tell me, 'Rake the lawn.' Five minutes later, she'd say it again. Three times and I was grounded. She'd yell and I'd say, 'Don't yell at me,' and we'd have a big argument. I hated her at first. All those restrictions!"

But one Sunday, sitting in church, the teenage boy looked over at his stepmother and thought, "She's really not that bad. Would I be upset if she died? Would I cry? Yes, I'd probably cry. I'd be upset." His stepmother still yells, but he likes her now, so it doesn't bother him as much as it once did. What about all those restrictions? "They're still around, but I guess it's good for me to be more organized."[10]

Some stepparents who try to exert control—and fail—lash out at their spouse. When Dave and Maria married, all was well until Maria's daughter, Toni, began to experience the pangs of adolescent rebellion. She broke some house rules, she argued with Dave and Maria, and all her distrust came pouring out. Dave reacted strongly, telling Maria, "I married you, not your kid." He packed a suitcase and left home for a couple of nights, and Maria ended up sending Toni to live with her biological father.

What Dave did not understand was that Toni's rebellion was normal. He expected unquestioning obedience, and when he didn't get it, he assumed it was because he was "only a stepfather." But teenagers disobey biological fathers, too. Dave allowed his personal feelings and pride to disrupt the united front he and Maria should have presented to Toni. As a result, Maria was wounded twice, by her husband and by her daughter; and Toni was uprooted from the home she had known for years.

Dr. Hetherington recommends that step-in parents of teenagers be high in warmth, responsiveness, and communication, and that they monitor children's activities without demanding unquestioning obedience.[11]

Jorge Escobar is a step-in dad for two teenage boys, and he enjoys parenting teenagers. "The boys were well-behaved, and they respected their mother when I married her," Jorge recalls. "It was an easy transition because she raised them well. My job now, since they're already formed, is to help knock off some rough edges. Because they are teens, it's a polishing process.

"They're good boys, and I thank God for them. I contributed nothing to them. I can't take credit for their talents, but I can appreciate them for who they are and try to encourage them and build them up. I just want them to become the men God wants them to be."

GROWN CHILDREN

What happens when families merge and some, if not all, of the children are mature? Barbara Wilson and her three brothers and sisters were grown and out of the house when their father married again. Barbara's new "stepmother," a lovely widow, also had four grown children about the ages of Barbara and her siblings. Together, they should have been eight young adults with a lot in common. But they weren't—and their story shows how much potential for hurt there is when families merge. If adults feel this way, imagine how kids must feel!

One of the first problems was that in both families there was a girl named Kathy. "They don't need me anymore; they already have a Kathy," sobbed Barbara's thirty-year-old sister. Seriously.

A major problem arose because Barbara's father moved into his new wife's house. "There's a huge territorial thing," Barbara says. "Since all the kids have grown up and moved away, we all want to come home to a sense of security. We lost our home and our mother. But at Thanksgiving my stepsister came home and threw a fit because there was a television—my father's—in the living room. 'We don't have a television in our living room,' she said. 'We've never had a television in the living room.'

"Of course, I knew she wasn't really upset about the television, but about all the people who have moved into her house," Barbara adds. "She was married and had her own family, but she wanted things to be the same when she came home. And they weren't."

No, they weren't—but her father tried desperately

to keep them the same. Barbara says that he didn't want to part with any of his furniture, thinking that his kids would at least feel comfortable with the same furnishings, so he moved all his furniture into his new wife's house. "There are three couches in the living room," Barbara says, "and two pianos, side by side. Her kids play their piano, and my father's kids play ours. There are two easy chairs side by side. Worst of all, my dad's furniture is olive and orange, while hers is green and gold."

The family faces a continual problem with merging traditions. "While we were growing up, we put these really nice stockings under the Christmas tree," Barbara says. "And my stepmother wants us to hang across the fireplace these ugly red and white stockings with our names written in glitter. We feel that we've simply lost our Christmas traditions. Dad keeps trying to introduce new traditions, which only makes everyone feel more lost, and no one knows when to open presents, where to hang stockings, or who bakes what kind of pie.

"I'm not really close to my in-laws, but my husband and I have decided to spend Christmas with his folks from now on," Barbara admits. "It's more like a family Christmas and less like a fraternity. It's not that we don't like my father's wife. She's a really good stepmother. But we just don't feel like a real family anymore. There are no traditional family expectations when you try to merge two families that have already grown up. There's no history there, and to expect sibling bonding is impossible.

"She says I'm like a daughter to her, but it's just not

the same and I don't expect it to be. There are just too many of us for her to make a commitment to us."

SPECIAL STRESSES

Integrating two households into one or bringing someone from another family into yours brings special stresses. Foster children come from extremely dysfunctional families with no clear expectations or proper role models. They don't know what families are supposed to be, and their actions are unpredictable.

Single parents run their homes differently than do married couples, says Dr. Martin Goldberg, director of the Marriage Council of Philadelphia. "Single parents tend to develop systems that are very communal and democratic. For better or worse, kids are voting equally with the parent. Or sometimes the kids have taken over as the controlling force. Neither way will work in a second marriage. The new spouse is going to object and will fight the amount of control the kids have, but often that spouse won't take a strong stand or move to establish a new system."[12]

Likewise, a foster child or grandchild from a one-parent family is likely to resent losing power when he or she moves into a two-parent family.

FINANCIAL STRAINS

As a step-in parent, you must be a careful money manager. It takes the average stepfamily at least four years to adjust to each other, and money is a big part of the adjustment. "Money is a loaded issue in stepfamilies," explains sociologist Constance Ahrons. "There so often are ongoing financial obligations that you don't find in a first marriage."[13]

Why is money such an issue? Because a man with children is probably paying child support to his first wife. A woman with children will be involved with raising them and may be contributing to their expenses. When children come to visit their noncustodial parent, he or she may take them out and splurge large amounts of money on them, upsetting the other children and the present spouse.

Mark Bruce Rosin, a stepfather and author of *Stepfathering*, says, "Stepfamily members, often uneasy at best in their new relationships, may conclude that money goes where the heart goes. The stepmother who complains about her husband's splurging on his visiting son, for example, might really feel that she and her family are being deprived of his full commitment." [14]

Many stepparents who pool their resources into one family "pot" may feel resentful when their hard-earned money is spent on an ungracious and unappreciative kid. "It's hard to give to children who aren't treating you well," says Dr. Patricia Papernow, research chair of the National Board of the Stepfamily Association of America, "but it's easier if you're appreciated by their parent. When a man resents helping support his stepchildren after agreeing to do it, it's sometimes a sign that the kids aren't the only ones who are not treating him well; his wife may not be appreciating him enough."[15]

Some experts suggest that fathers who must make

child support payments do so from a separate account, thus sparing the wife the pang of seeing money flow out of the family.

Other problems can be solved by carefully planning a budget. If the stepchildren are coming for a visit, plan a realistic budget to cover their increased expenses and *stick to it*. If you feel that your spouse's financial support of noncustodial children is keeping you from meeting a financial goal for your family—a new house, for instance—then make a realistic plan of saving for the new house that can coexist with the child support payments.

Whatever you do, talk openly about financial concerns. Don't let hidden bitterness weaken your relationship and cause resentment. And remember that God has promised to supply all your needs if you are seeking him and his kingdom.

Money is often a special strain when grandparents are raising grandchildren. Grandparents may be spending their long-saved pensions or retirement funds on their grandchildren. They don't want to endanger their future, but they don't know how else to provide for the children. Money is an ever-present concern.

But God can provide, no matter what your situation. I interviewed Mary Ann Kuharski, mother of thirteen children. "How do you afford such a large family?" I asked, thinking of how tight the budget can be stretched even with my two kids.

"Well, my husband works for the county, so we're not rich and we don't get fat bonuses. When we first started out, our budget was stretched and we had to take out two loans," she explained. "We started to pursue adoption without really having the financial wherewithal. It was a step in faith, something we thought was just a good idea. But God is never outdone in generosity. The minute we got more than six kids, people began giving us clothes, even *designer* clothes, for even my husband and me. We buy shoes and socks and underwear, but I can't remember the last time I had to buy a winter coat for a kid. We learned that if you say yes to God, he will clothe all your little sparrows.

"We do pinch pennies," Mary Ann said. "And my husband, John, buys groceries in quantity and uses coupons so he saves thirty or forty dollars each time."

I had to ask: "How large is your house?"

"Obviously the kids don't have rooms of their own," she said, "but we have five bedrooms, including one in the basement for three girls."

Each Kuharski child either works or has a paper route, and each pays half his private school tuition. It is understood that they will pay their way through college. "We all really pull together," said Mary Ann.

SEXUAL ISSUES

Some people would rather not talk about sexual issues within the blended family, but step-in parents need to think about how they will handle sexuality in the home. Step-in fathers, particularly, often feel uncomfortable with unrelated girls who live in their home. Teenage siblings may feel sexually attracted to one another. And no one needs to be reminded of how common sexual abuse is within stepfamilies and foster families.

Chuck and Andrea Peters married when Andrea's daughter, Tammy, was twelve. Tammy was so excited at the prospect of having a father in the home again that she called Chuck "Dad" right away. She longed for the attention and affection that her biological father no longer gave her.

But Tammy and her mother had grown close during Andrea's single years, and when Andrea remarried, Tammy felt left out. "I didn't really need her like before," Andrea says. "And Tammy was very lonely at times. She expressed these feelings to me, but as much as I tried, it just wasn't the same."

Tammy needed male affection, too, but Chuck did not know how to give it. He would hug her neck or pat her head, but he was never really comfortable giving physical affection to Tammy.

One morning Tammy jumped into bed with Chuck just as she used to do when her biological father lived at home. "There was nothing to it, except that she was looking for closeness," Andrea says, "but Chuck got up quickly, without making a big deal of it. He was embarrassed, but we both understood Tammy's doing it and felt sorry for her. She was crying out for male attention, and she had zero self-esteem."

"Tammy had been totally rejected by her [biological] father—not only did he leave home, but he made very few attempts to talk to her or see her. Though we loved her and would have done anything for her, we couldn't give her the male attention and affection she was seeking."

The awkwardness between Tammy and Chuck is common. Studies by James Bray and Mavis

Hetherington suggest that while girls appreciate verbal praise from step-in fathers, they are uncomfortable with physical gestures from these fathers. Bray says that step-in fathers often think they're giving "affection or praise when they hug the kids, but the girls often don't experience this as positive."

It wasn't that step-in fathers were "lusting after their stepdaughters," Hetherington says. "Both were just confused because there's no prescription for how to express normal affection to an unrelated girl."[16]

Pearl Prilik offers the following guidelines for dealing with sexuality in the blended family:

- Don't be afraid to set limits.
- Give opposite-sex stepsiblings separate bedrooms.
- Close bathroom doors when the bathroom is in use.
- Wear robes and cover-ups.
- Do not discuss individual sexual behavior except with a parent.
- Keep the parents' sexuality private.[17]

Once God brings you together with a child, each of you must find your own place in the relationship. Your roles will shift over time, as you grow mentally, spiritually, and emotionally. Growth pangs will come and go as you both change.

"Presume not that I am the thing I was," said Shakespeare's King Henry. After your time of loving someone else's child, neither of you will be quite what you once were. I hope your changing roles will bring you closer to what God would have each of you to be.

SEVEN
The Others Who Influence Your Family

The most important person in the world to me was my first-grade teacher. Since I didn't have a mom, I really looked up to her and she believed in me. She'd give all the other kids a couple of sentences to say in the school play, but to me she gave a whole paragraph. —Donald, age twenty-seven

I don't live with my stepmom, but I see her every Saturday. She is so nice to me. She never yells at me or anything. Maybe if I lived with her she would be different, but I don't think so. I think my stepmom is the greatest in the world. —Melanie, age eleven

The best thing about having stepparents is you have two dads or mothers who will be there if you have a problem. So if one of them can't fix your problem, the other one can. —Theresa, age eleven

When you step-in as a parent to a child, whether you do so as a stepparent, a foster parent, a grandparent, or a guardian, you are involving yourself not just in the life of one or more children, but in many other lives as well. The children have parents, grandparents, and other relatives whose influence will touch both you and the child.

THE TELEPHONE

When Christine and George Bartlett got married, they had to cope with frequent phone calls from George's ex-wife, Cathy. She called not only to talk about their daughter, but to get George's opinion on everything from medicine to household repairs. Though their marriage had ended some time before, Cathy still depended on George emotionally.

Perhaps the most common instrument used to irritate or harass step-in parents is the telephone. Telephone calls from one or both biological parents can be persistent, annoying, and rude. They can come in the middle of the night. "It was after I had a baby that my kids' mother began calling," one mother told me. "She told them I wouldn't love them anymore now that I had a baby."

Children can aggravate a step-in family situation by telephoning their noncustodial parent(s) every time something doesn't go their way in the new family. "Kids use the phone to make sympathy calls," a school guidance counselor told me. "Whenever something happens to make them upset with a step-in mom or dad, they call their noncustodial parent and cry on the phone. It makes things harder for everyone."

BITTER EX-SPOUSES

Often, bitter biological parents will try to deny that
the step-in parents even exist. They cannot bear the
thought that other people are influencing and shaping
their child's life.

Chuck and Andrea Peters married when they each
had teenage children. His ex-wife made things difficult
for the new family. Andrea recalls, "Every weekend
when the kids would visit us, they'd say, 'Mom's upset
we're not over there. We'd better go or we'll hear
about it.' Chuck's ex-wife did not want her children
to have another mother figure."

These outside influences cannot be ignored or
denied. Mark Bruce Rosin says that any parent who
steps in to raise someone else's children "must create
relationships with his partner and stepchildren not
on the basis of a clean slate but with the residue of
divorce or death as an aspect that must be acknowl-
edged."[1]

GHOSTS OF THE PAST

Emily and John Visher, authors of *How to Win as a
Stepfamily,* know that past relationships often over-
shadow the present. You may feel haunted by a previous relationship if you are dealing with an ex-spouse.
The Vishers say:

> You may be unable to separate from the past.
> Because of this, the people in your new house-
> hold unit may feel that you are not truly commit-
> ted to your stepfamily unit. Your present spouse
> may feel unappreciated and insecure; your

children may continue to act in all sorts of annoying ways because they hope they can somehow
reverse things and bring back "the good old
days" as they remember them; and your stepchildren may feel rejected by you if you hold yourself
back from relating to them because your guilt creates a barrier. You may even feel guilty that you
can provide material and emotional gifts to your
stepchildren that you are unable to give to your
biological children.

Your guilt also may lead you to try to keep your
ex-spouse from being angry, and often this leads
to trouble in your new household. Your present
spouse may get the feeling that his or her feelings
count much less to you than the feelings of your
former spouse.[2]

If you are dealing with an ex-spouse when you make
arrangements for your children, try to establish a
physical and emotional distance between the two
households. The Vishers suggest that you separate
from your ex-spouse psychologically. Put a limit on
telephone conversations and letters. Don't depend on
him or her as you did when you were married. Don't
wait for his or her approval when you make a decision. Your life must go on independently or with your
new spouse.[3] Don and Judy Howe of Chicago raised
three children from his previous marriage. "We
thought we had done everything right beforehand by
including the kids in our activities," Judy recalls.
"They were even in the wedding party. But we hadn't
anticipated loyalty conflicts. Once the new household

was set up, their biological mother told them that they couldn't call me their stepmother because she was still alive. The kids picked up the signals. None of us had realized how the losses we were all facing would have to be dealt with."[4]

Step-in parents who routinely deal with the children's biological parents share some common gripes:

"Why do the kids come home in rags when I sent them out in nice clothes?"

"Why can't their father pick them up on time? And sometimes I'm out of my head worrying when he's late bringing them home."

"My wife and I made plans for the weekend because the kids were supposed to be visiting their mother, but she called at the last minute and canceled. Not only has that wrecked our plans, but I've got to tell the kids their mother is too busy for them this weekend."

"I hate sending my grandkids to visit their parents. When they come home, my kids have told my grandkids all sorts of crazy stories about how mean I was when I was raising them. It's just not fair."

BIOLOGICAL PARENTS

How can you deal with the sometimes prickly influence of a biological mother or father? First, if the biological parents want to spend time alone with their children and such contact has not been legally prohibited for some reason, let the children spend time with them. If for some reason I wasn't able to rear *my* children, I'd be prickly, too. If I couldn't have custody of them, I'd want to know someone loved and cared—

a lot—for them. I'd want time with them to make sure they knew I was their mother and that I loved them. Try to put yourself in the biological parent's situation and imagine how you would feel.

Don't downplay the influence of the child's other parent. Mark Rosin is a step-in father who believes that the more active a child's biological father is in the child's life, "the less likely our stepchildren will need us to play a predominantly father-figure role for them, and the less support we'll get from them if we are inclined to try to play this role. This is especially true if our stepchildren live full time with their father and only visit with their mother and us."[5]

If your child's biological parent is a regular and active presence in his or her life, don't try to usurp that position. "We must make clear to ourselves and to our stepchildren," says Rosin, "that we are not attempting to take the place of their biological fathers [or mothers], to take over the unique relationships they have with them, or to eradicate their memories of them."[6] Though you may be fatherlike or motherlike, says Rosin, you are still a step-in parent unless you legally adopt the child. This is equally true for grand-parents, foster parents, and other guardians.

If the child's biological parents are completely out of the scene, however, you may find that your role is virtually identical to that of biological parents. A recent Father's Day column in "Dear Abby" paid special tribute to those men who stepped into a family whose "real" father "died, disappeared, or was just not around for one of a thousand reasons."[7] The same tribute is due to step-in mothers.

ABSENT PARENTS

Unfortunately for many thousands of children, divorced fathers often disappear from their children's lives. In a study at the University of Pennsylvania, researchers investigated fathers who did not have custody of their children and found that contact between divorced fathers and their children diminishes sharply over time. Only 10 percent of the children had regular contact with their fathers when first interviewed, and only 5 percent reported regular contact when interviewed five years later. The study noted that "the drop-off in father-child contact is especially evident among children whose fathers moved out when they were quite young—many of whom lose contact with their fathers for most or all of childhood."[8]

Even an absent parent can influence a household. Remember the story *Rebecca* by Daphne du Maurier? Rebecca, Max de Winter's first wife, had been dead for some time, but his new bride felt her influence everywhere in the old family estate: from the embossed initialed stationery, to the exquisite furniture Rebecca had chosen, even to her new husband's melancholy behavior whenever Rebecca's name was mentioned. The new Mrs. de Winter was racked with worry and insecurity, all because Rebecca's foreboding influence hovered all around her, or so she thought.

Our perception of people, even if incorrect, may influence us more than the reality. If a child's biological parent has died or disappeared, he or she may think of the absent parent as a saint, a hero, or a villain, and that perception will influence how he accepts a step-in parent.

Allow children time to grieve. Grief has many stages and each person reacts to it differently. Sometimes we just have to feel bad until we don't feel that way anymore. God understands that we need time to pull ourselves back together.

Try not to make the absent parent into a saint. Children have a tendency to do that anyway, so don't encourage it. Let the children keep their fond memories of happy times, and don't criticize the biological parent, but don't hide the person's faults, either. Be honest. If the deceased parent is portrayed as having been perfectly wonderful, no earthly step-in parent can ever compete.

Don't describe or think of yourself as one who will replace the parent who has died. We all deserve to be loved for who we are, not for whose shoes we are trying to fill.

GRANDPARENTS

Let's take a moment to talk about grandparents—not grandparents who are raising their grandchildren, but your parents, the grandparents of your biological children, if you have any, and the step-in grandparents of the children you are choosing to love.

Since 1978, when retired Atlanta real estate developer Mike Goldgar ended his successful six-year campaign to have Congress recognize grandparents in a legal holiday,[9] much public attention has been focused on grandparents clamoring for their rights to visit with their grandchildren. Why is being a grandparent such a big deal? For those of us who aren't grandparents yet, Andrew Cherlin and Frank Furstenberg, Jr., explain:

> Becoming a grandparent is a deeply meaningful event in a person's life. Seeing the birth of grandchildren can give a person a great sense of the completion of being, of immortality through the chain of generations. It is an affirmation of the value of one's life and, at the same time, a hedge against death. Grandchildren are also a great source of personal pleasure.[10]

Given how much grandchildren mean to grandparents, it is truly a tragedy that when parents divorce, children will most likely never see their paternal grandparents again. British researchers Janet Finch and Jennifer Mason investigated grandparent-grandchild relationships after divorce and discovered that these relationships were "a relatively minor consideration" for the majority of the divorced mothers they interviewed. In many cases, they write, "the link between grandparent and grandchild seems to have been 'lost' as an inevitable consequence of [the divorced mother's] wanting to sever all ties with the former spouse."[11]

If biological grandchildren are important because they affirm "immortality through the chain of generations," how are grandparents to react to stepgrandchildren? The sense of continuing life experienced with the birth of a biological grandchild is absent when stepgrandchildren arrive on the scene. There are two key factors in how well stepgrandchildren and stepgrandparents get along: the age of the stepgrandchild at the time he or she first became a member of the grandparent's extended family, and whether the stepgrandchild lived full-time with the grandparent's adult child.[12]

A survey of grandparents found that one-third of the respondents agreed with statements such as "Your stepgrandchildren can't think of you as a real grandparent," "It is harder for you to be a stepgrandparent than a grandparent," or "You feel differently about your natural grandchildren than your stepgrandchildren." Fifty-six percent agreed with "You tend to see less of your stepgrandchildren."[13]

Why aren't grandparents closer to their stepgrandchildren? One reason may be that stepgrandchildren have at least three sets of grandparents, and many have many more. It is hard for kids to have deep and meaningful relationships with stepgrandparents, especially if they haven't yet learned to trust the new family. They don't want to take the emotional risk of losing a grandparent again.

But grandparents can play an active role in the nurture of their children's stepchildren, no matter how the kids came to be in the family. For this to work, however, the grandparents must live close to the family, and they must see the children and parents frequently. "It also helps if the grandparents are younger," say Cherlin and Furstenberg, authors of *The New American Grandparent*. Youthful grandparents "are better able to cope physically with the duties of caring for children."

What can grandparents do to make things better for the new families? How can they function as step-in grandparents?

First, grandparents should realize that a difficult situation can easily be made worse if they build walls instead of bridges. Emily and John Visher give these points for stepgrandparents to consider. Many of them apply to foster or adoptive grandparents also.

Grandparents can build walls:

- by not welcoming their child's new spouse into their home
- by not welcoming the "new" kids into their home
- by not acknowledging the new marriage
- by sabotaging the new marriage
- by unequally treating grandchildren and stepgrandchildren
- by pointing out which children are biologically related
- by doting on a new grandchild
- by commenting that your job is "too difficult"

Grandparents can build bridges:

- by recognizing that stepgrandparents are important to stepgrandkids
- by learning how their child's stepfamily wants them to relate to the grandkids
- by doing fun things with all the children
- by creating new traditions for a new stepfamily
- by being a safe place in a storm
- by supporting the adults in the family[14]

As step-in parents, you can make things easier for grandparents by arranging times when grandparents and kids can do things together as they did before the family changed. You can arrange private times when step-in grandparents and new children in the family can get to know each other. Have a family reunion and play icebreaker games! Include your parents in some of your new family's special events, and from time to time, include your parents in adult activities without the kids. If you have remarried, give them time to get to know and accept your spouse.

Grandparents can be a blessing or a burden. Denise had a seven-year-old daughter when she married Mark, and Mark's parents seemed to accept her child. But when Mark and Denise's baby, Ryan, was born, Mark's parents went bananas over the new baby. Denise was hurt—they had never shown that much excitement over her daughter. Did they love her seven-year-old less than they loved Ryan?

Eventually Denise's feelings erupted in a big argument with her mother-in-law. For three months the two families did not speak to one another and the grandparents didn't see the grandchildren at all. Then the grandparents agreed to show equal attention to each child. Denise and Mark were lucky—some families fight and the grandparents are forever separated from their grandchildren.

How can grandparents or step-in grandparents who live far from their grandchildren find ways to be part of the children's lives? Grandparents can correspond with grandchildren. Even little children love to receive letters. When grandparents travel, they can send postcards. Year-round they can send birthday cards, special holiday greetings, and newsy notes.

Grandparents can telephone their grandchildren on occasion. Even if the children are too shy or embarrassed to talk at first, at least they'll know their grandparents cared enough to ask for them. But thoughtful grandparents will check with the child's parents before calling, or the telephone can rapidly become an irritation.

Children and grandparents can exchange tapes— video or audio. Years ago my mother, aunts, and grandmother sat down in the living room with a cassette tape recorder, and Grandma sang all the old songs she used to sing on the front porch of their home in Alabama. I still have that tape, and it's precious. I enjoy not only the songs, but the conversation and banter between songs. Now that so many families have video cameras, your children can have a visual as well as audio remembrance of their grandparents. Why not ask your parents to send videotapes through the mail as "talking postcards" and let the kids make a tape to send back?

Grandparents should try to keep up with their grandchildren's interests. A notebook with a separate page listing each grandchild's name, age, birthday, and interests would be a good gift for grandparents. The kids can then write letters to Grandma and Grandpa that will fit right into the notebook.

When grandparents visit, try to encourage activities that will make memories. Don't just opt for sitting around the house or going to an amusement park. Suggest that the grandparents take the kids to a downtown drugstore that has a lunch counter. Encourage kids and grandparents to go for a walk in the park and feed squirrels. Perhaps your mom or dad could teach the kids a skill that they enjoy and you don't: quilting, fishing, knitting, carpentry, or whatever.

Grandparents will not always agree with the way parents are raising the children. Sometimes grandparents and parents play tug of war in the areas of discipline and tradition. They may disagree on bedtime, manners, chores, and nutrition. Other tensions may rise when grandparents want children to follow an old tradition that the parents reject. If compromise is not possible, says Dr. Arthur Kornhaber, author of *Between Parents and Grandparents*, "the parents' wishes should rule because the child lives with the parents, and grandparents should understand that."[15]

KEEPING OUTSIDERS OUT OF YOUR HAIR

When outside influences disrupt or overwhelm your family, you have the right and the responsibility to call a halt to the problem. Gerald Weeks, director of clinical training at the Marriage Council of Philadelphia, suggests a systematic approach for keeping outsiders in their place:

> First, ask yourself who is involved with your family besides your husband and your children. Who do you think about? Who do you worry about? Who is a part of your daily activity? One simple way to answer these questions is to look at your daily routine. Is there someone you call or someone who calls you every day or every week? Until you really examine your activities, you don't realize how many people are part of your life, or in what way they're involved, or that intrusions are even taking place.

The next step is to examine your thoughts about those intrusions.

> Look at what you're thinking about when your mother calls—not what you're feeling, what you're *thinking*. Are you thinking that your mother can't take care of herself and that something will happen to her if you don't stay in close touch? Or, if it's your ex-spouse who's calling, are you allowing him to intrude because you're still seeking his approval? Once you discover why you let these intrusions continue, you can do something about them.[16]

Therapists recommend that the person most directly connected to the outsider then approach the person. When Denise and Mark had problems with his parents, it should have been Mark who approached them, not Denise. Couples should try to negotiate with difficult outsiders, firmly setting standards and boundaries on their time, the interaction with the children, and what can be done (and bought!) for the children. "It's tough," says Dr. Martin Goldberg, "because when people divorce and remarry, nobody really leaves the family system. You just add more people, and they're not going to go away."[17]

Sometimes negative influences cannot be removed or negotiated. Marilee Kastle takes her two foster children to supervised visits with their biological parents once a month. "The children will wet the bed the night after the visit," she says. "They seemed confused at first, but now they don't really care if they see their biological parents or not. In fact, the boy prefers not to see them at all, but is required to go by the government. The little girl does not remember anything bad about them and sees her mother as her mother—nothing else. These parents have no emotional hold on these children."

"Contact with biological parents can be painful," another foster mother told me. "It's so confusing. The homes are probably *so* different. Our foster son was with us for the first three years of his life and we were his family. Then when he started extended visits with his biological parents, he was told we were horrid people."

When you or your child has an unpleasant encounter with one of the "outsiders" in your life, help your child feel secure in your love and in your home. Remind him that he is a person of worth, created by a loving God who has his best interests at heart. We live in an imperfect world and sometimes there are bad things in our lives, but God can use all things for our good. We can grow stronger. If we trust and rest in him, we cannot and will not be out of his care.

CAREER SUCCESS: A SEDUCTIVE OUTSIDER

There is an unlikely outside influence that may prevent you from successfully loving someone else's child: success. In America, home of free enterprise, haven of the entrepreneur, and birthplace of the yuppie, it is easy to get caught up in the consuming drive for career success.

Is the drive for career success dangerous? Are the rewards that success brings worth the stresses it places on marriages and families? Men and women addicted to the pursuit of success often forfeit happy homes and stable marriages for a series of insignificant moments and pleasures that quickly fade. Actress Liv Ullman warns that "the best thing that can come with success is the knowledge that it is nothing to long for."[18]

There is nothing inherently wrong with success, of course, but those who pursue it at all costs place their families and marriages in danger. Nancy Austin and Tom Peters, authors of the best-selling *Passion for Excellence,* admit that most of the success-oriented people they know have given up "family vacations, Little League games, birthday dinners, evenings, weekends and lunch hours, gardening, reading, movies, and most other pastimes. We have a number of friends whose marriages crumbled under the weight of their devotion to a dream. There are more newly single parents than we expected among our colleagues."

Austin and Peters say they are frequently asked if it is possible to have full and satisfying personal and professional lives; their answer is no. "The price of excellence is time, energy, attention, and focus. . . . Excellence is a high-cost item."

Is excellence more important than relationships? No! Pat and Jill Williams, who tell their story in *Rekindled* (Revell, 1985), seemed to have a perfect marriage. Pat was famous, the general manager of the Philadelphia 76ers, an author, a renowned motivational speaker. But his identity was wrapped up in what he did for a living and how well he did it. Consumed by the quest for excellence, he would do anything to get the job done. Although he didn't realize it at the time, that included sacrificing his marriage and family.

More than anything, Jill Williams wanted to adopt a child. Pat had heard her express that desire for many years, but he never really gave it serious consideration until the day he realized her love for him had simply died. He had neglected her and her deepest heartfelt desire for so long that she was emotionally empty.

Pat began to rebuild his marriage with the same zeal he applied to his business. He realized that Jill's desire to love more children was not simply a whim, but an urgent need. Together they considered adoption, and together they added children to their family. Their latest child, a girl adopted from Romania, arrived in May 1991.

Pat and Jill now have a thriving marriage. Pat is still committed to excellence (he is the president and general manager of the newest NBA team, the Orlando Magic), but he now commits time to his wife and thirteen children. He has found a way to make time for Little League games, trips to the beach, softball in the back yard, and quiet evenings out with his wife. He knows that although a man or woman can be devoted to excellence in family *and* business, if the two are kept in balance, ultimately marriage and family are more important.

Too often we confuse the urgent with the important. Urgent things, such as meetings, flat tires, and overdrawn bank accounts, mean little or nothing in the eternal scheme of things. But your toddler's first nightmare, your teenager's first date, and your spouse's enduring dreams are important.

Urgent things clamor loudly and demand our attention. Important things are often quiet and unobtrusive.

Urgent things are many. Important things are few.

Urgent things can be solved by quick action. Important things require careful, thoughtful attention.

Are you addicted to success? Are you giving too much attention to things that won't really matter in a few years? If you make a sincere commitment to love someone else's child, you'll have to measure your desire for success in that commitment against your need for success in other areas. In the final analysis, which is more important?

HELPFUL HINTS

Though you may not be the children's biological or even legal parent, you still have responsibilities and you deserve respect. No matter how you arrived at your situation, if you have custody of the children, you are in charge of their welfare. You are responsible for your own actions and attitudes. You don't have to listen to harsh, unmerited criticism. You don't have to feel inferior. God has brought these children into your life for a reason, and you are the person he wants to use now. Take confident charge of that responsibility.

If you are married, don't expect to raise these children alone. Don't "take over" for your husband or your wife, especially if your spouse is the children's biological parent. When two parents are present, parenting should be an equal partnership.

As a step-in parent, don't feel you have to compete for the title of Mom or Dad. You don't have to prove yourself by doing or buying or being something that you wouldn't ordinarily do or buy or be. You are who you are, and you should try to be the best parent you can be. But you cannot and should not compete with the child's biological parent or anyone else outside your home.

Realize, too, that like everyone else, kids have a way of taking those who support them for granted. You may find that you are spending more time and money on this child than someone else who comes along and captures his attention and affection. Don't become discouraged or resentful. Kids go through phases of hero worship, and few of us really appreciate what we had at home until after we leave it.

As you love someone else's child, don't dwell on the past or the future. Forget about how an outsider has hurt your pride. Like rare treasures, bring out the good memories and savor them; remember the lessons from the painful times. But don't dwell on yesterday, and don't hold the past and the influences of others against the child who lives with you.

Likewise, remember that only God knows what next year will bring. The future will certainly bring change to your home, whether it's a change in custody arrangements, or the birth of a new baby. Foster care ends. Children often return to their original homes. Both young and old die.

So live each day to its fullest extent, enjoying your home and the children in your care. Be the best you can be, and ask what God would have you do today.

EIGHT
Understanding a Child's Sense of Loss and Loyalty

The frustrating part of living in a "mixed" family is seeing this person and no matter how much they try to be your parent, you don't see them as a parent. I see my stepmom as sort of a stranger, and that is hard because I really try hard not to, but I just can't help it. —Mark, age fourteen

I like having a stepdad because you have a bigger family, but sometimes it's not so great when they have kids because then my mom and stepdad fight about paying to get my younger stepsister [child support] and it's just no fun at all! —Heather, age thirteen

I have a big problem with calling my stepmom "Mom." Also, my dad always seems to stick up for her all the time. —Melissa, age thirteen

My biggest challenge is remembering that my stepfather is not there to take my real dad's place. Although my stepdad is like a real father, I

still love both of my fathers the same. —Greg,
age thirteen

My greatest challenge is calling my stepfather "Dad" and also giving him the same
amount of love that I give my mom. —Bill,
age fifteen

The worst thing I think about is that my dad
doesn't love my mom. —Mary, age twelve

"Stepchildren feel like there is a card game and they
have been dealt out," says columnist Erma Bombeck,
who became a stepdaughter at age eleven, two years
after the death of her father. "You feel like you have
nothing to play, no choice, no say in anything. I was
angry. My mother did all the right things to prepare
me. But I felt like the person who goes to a Broadway
play expecting to see someone famous and finds out
that an understudy will be taking the role. I wanted my
real father or no father at all."

Erma desperately wanted a class ring in high school.
Her mother refused to buy one, but at the last minute,
the ring appeared. Erma thanked her mother, who
said, "I didn't buy it. Your father bought it."

Erma says she thought, *Why did he do this?* I loved
him for it, and I half resented him."

Bombeck says it took between five and ten years
before she and her stepfather began to feel comfortable with one another. "It has worked out so well at
this point," she says, "I cannot remember what my
natural father looked like. It's this man who raised me
who is so important."[1]

CHILDREN ARE PULLED APART

"Because children are part of two biological parents they nearly always have very strong pulls to other parents," say John and Emily Visher, authors of *How to Win as a Stepfamily*. "These divided loyalties often make it difficult for children to relate comfortably to all the parental adults in their lives. Rejection of a stepparent, for example, may have nothing to do with the personal characteristics of the stepparent. In fact, warm and loving stepparents may cause especially severe loyalty conflicts for children. As children and adults are able to accept the fact that children can care for more than two parental adults, then the children's loyalty conflicts can diminish and the new steprelationships improve." The Vishers say it may help the children for step-in parents to acknowledge negative as well as positive feelings about ex-spouses, but then children may become caught in loyalty conflicts and feel insecure if specific critical remarks are made continually about their other parent.[2]

If a child genuinely likes the new step-in parent, she may feel guilty. She feels that loyalty to her biological mother or father somehow requires that she dislike her step-in parent. "There isn't a stepchild worth his salt who doesn't have some loyalty conflicts," says Dr. Judith S. Wallerstein, executive director of the Center for the Family in Transition in Corte Madera, California.[3]

Lesley Dormen was seven when her mother remarried, and Lesley grew to love her stepfather. "He was handsome and affectionate, and I was crazy about him," she says. "Not that life was one long party. He had a temper, and there were plenty of family crises. But that's just it—we were a family."

When Lesley's biological father came to visit, "he seemed like an exotic celebrity, a stranger I felt some mysterious tie to," she says. "His visits confused and saddened me. Although my head grasped the logistics and complications of divorce, on some deeper level I was wondering, *Hey, I have a dad, so who is* this *guy?* I also felt guilty. Was I disloyal to my real father for liking my stepdad so much? I thought I saw rejection in my father's eyes, and I wanted to protect him from that feeling. Could I?"[4]

Children of an alcoholic or unfit parent may have particular difficulty adjusting to a step-in parent or a new family. "Children often feel protective of and responsible for a so-called 'weak' parent," says Patricia Papernow, a Massachusetts psychotherapist.[5] Most foster families, in fact, are given special training to understand children's loyalty conflicts in this situation.

NO LIMIT TO LOVE

If you think your child may be trapped by loyalty to an absent parent, reassure him that love is limitless. Just as God loves each person very, very much, so your child can learn to love each adult in his life in a different way. He has only one biological mother and father, but God may send other very special people into his life. God will even act as his Father, for he promises to be a "father to the fatherless" (Psalm 68:5).

Family therapist Ann Getzoff tells kids that it's okay

to like a step-in parent: "That does not mean that you like your own parent any less. You've simply found a new friend, and that's okay."

Getzoff advises that if biological parents seem upset that the child likes her step-in parent, "try to put that message in perspective. Your parent is insecure and jealous, and while those feelings are painful for your parent, they remain your parent's problem to solve."[6]

Kids also should know that it is normal for their feelings to vacillate wildly. They may simply adore a step-in mom or dad as long as the relationship is based on friendship: doing things together, laughing, having fun. But if the adult tries to "parent" the child by using discipline or enforcing a curfew, the child may be ready for the step-in parent to step out.

Such feelings are natural, and parents can and should talk about them with kids old enough to understand. "I'm not just here for the good times," a step-in parent should explain. "I'm here for the tough times, too."

THE RISK OF LOVING A STEP-IN PARENT

Besides the guilt children may feel over loving step-in parents, they also may hesitate to love because they fear losing this new parental figure. *If I love this person, will she leave me, too?* a child may wonder. Or *What will happen if this man dies and leaves us?* Children who are being raised by their grandparents worry particularly about their grandparents dying.

Children from disrupted families know that love is risky. By the time you step into their lives, they have already undergone at least one trauma. They may want you to guarantee that you will be in their lives forever.

As human beings, we can't do that. No one can predict what the future will bring. Those of you who are stepping in as foster parents know from the beginning that your relationship is temporary.

But children need security. They need to feel that they belong somewhere. So what can you do? You can promise that you will always love and care for them, that you will always welcome them into your home. You can reassure the child that he is special to you and no one can take his place. You can take the time to build a strong relationship with this child and teach him that no matter what happens in life, God is an ever-present father. His love and protection keep his children safely in his hand, even when we can't see his plan for us.

Mignon Scherer, founder of Grandparents Raising Grandchildren, has seen children torn between loyalty to parents and loyalty to grandparents. "If the children are very young and there isn't visitation with the parents, then it's not complicated," she says. "But if there's visitation, for the child it's like living in two worlds. Children find it difficult to exhibit one behavior in one home and another behavior in another home. Different things are expected in each place, and the children don't know how to turn it off from one place to another."[7]

Scherer has found that the issue of divided loyalty can grow stronger as the children grow older. If a visit to the biological parent's home does not go well, children often feel insecure after returning to their custodial home, leaving the step-in parents to deal with a child's shattered self-image.

"Children of a broken home have to work through a lot of pain and anger and make decisions about their feelings for their father and mother," says Andrea Peters, a stepmother. "Many of them question their faith in God. They feel the pain of their grieving mother or father. They worry, they feel insecure. All this suffering often causes bad behavior. They *need* affection, understanding, a listening ear, security, and sometimes professional counseling. If the custodial parent remarries, he or she must be sure the stepparent is mature, willing to sacrifice for the good of the children, caring, and loving. It really helps if the stepparent is a parent, too."

Andrea gently adds, "Even though my husband's adult children have told me they do not like me, they resent my children and grandchildren, they are not comfortable in our home, and they have been unappreciative of the many things I have done for them, I treat them with the love of Christ and welcome them to our home. I could not do this myself, but it is Christ who lives in me. I'm happier because my husband loves me the more for it and because I can pray with faith believing that one day they too will become committed Christians. God gives me a real peace."

CHILDREN FEEL STRIFE

Bob Dinkel and his second wife, Sharon Hanna, taped a "Good Morning America" broadcast with Bob's first wife, Karen, and her present husband, Jerry Baxter. Bob and Karen, though divorced, continued to fight with one another, usually about the children, Jeff and Greg. The boys lived with Bob but remained in contact with Karen. Greg told *McCall's* magazine, "Each parent only wanted to hear bad things about the other, so I didn't say anything."

The rift between the adults affected the children tremendously. Sharon's two daughters, Lisa and Lyn, were drawn into the fight. "Our house became very emotional," Lisa recalls. "My sister and I were unaccustomed to the screaming that went on in phone calls between Karen and Bob. Our own mother and father, though divorced, have always been able to talk to one another. And there were times when the boys sided with their mother, whereas we would always jump to the defense of our mother and Bob. That would create more tension."

When the two couples agreed to tape "Good Morning America," they had no idea how to solve their problems. But as they talked, they began to listen to their children. Greg said, "You feel so torn. You love both your parents and it's so hard when you're in the middle." Greg cried. The camera crew cried. People all across America realized how traumatic it is when children are torn between two parents they love.[8]

Emily Visher stresses that it is important for parents to cooperate in arrangements concerning the children. "For one thing," she says, "it gets children out of the middle between people they care about who are fighting with one another." She knows of one nine-year-old boy who said, "They're shooting arrows at one another, and the arrows go right through me."[9]

All families undergo struggles, but healthy families develop skills to meet conflicts as they arise. They work together to resolve problems that show signs of straining family life, including feelings of failure and guilt.[10]

When one person in a strong family has a problem, other family members sit and talk about it. It is our problem, not merely yours. They behave as if they believe in the old proverb: Sorrow shared is halved, joy shared is doubled. Strong families know they can handle problems because they have handled them in the past.

CHILDREN'S LOSSES

The children who come into your home have experienced their own losses, many of which may be too deep for words. Their struggles can include moving to a new location, leaving old friends, saying good-bye to grandparents; losing a mother or father through death, divorce, or abandonment; giving up dreams and expectations that the original family would be reunited; losing a daily child/parent relationship; losing a familiar community, school, and job; and losing a familiar role in the family.

Try to find out as much as you can about your child's situation through indirect sources: a social worker, a biological parent, another relative. Then, knowing his or her past, do your best to ease the pain of the child's loss by acknowledging that loss and helping the child to move on.

Janice Michaelson told me about Jesse, a four-year-old foster child she had raised for eight months. About three weeks after Jesse was moved into his grandparents' home in another state, his grandmother called Janice and said the boy wanted to talk to her. Somehow he had decided that his entire foster family had died.

"Mommy?" Jesse asked on the phone.

"Yes, Jesse. I'm here."

"Where are you?"

"I'm at home."

"Where is Daddy?"

"He's here, too."

"And Tommy and Terri and Michael?"

"They're all here."

"Okay. 'Bye."

Jesse felt so uprooted and lost he had to call his foster family to make sure they were still there. Their home was the most stable place he had ever known.

COMMUNICATION IS THE KEY

If your family is going to pull together and overcome each individual's sense of loss, you must communicate. Good communication doesn't just happen; it takes time and practice. Families have to talk about the unimportant things before they feel comfortable talking about the important things.

One way to encourage communication with older children is through regular family meetings. "Family meetings," says Marilyn Winter-Tamkins, a social worker in family therapy, "are a wonderful way of building unity. Don't have them just when problems occur, but spend time on deciding where to go on Sunday afternoon, who should be doing what chores, as well as talking about difficulties. It's important that everybody gets a chance to talk."

Family members also should validate one another, Winter-Tamkins says. "We encourage people to do this on a daily basis, find two or three things they can compliment each stepfamily member on to build a feeling of good will."[11]

COMMUNICATING ONE-ON-ONE

Step-in parents must establish communication on a one-on-one basis with the children. They are at a disadvantage because they usually haven't been around during the child's formative years. A step-in mother doesn't know, for instance, that when Johnny says, "I don't have a drink," he really means, "Will you pour me a drink?" A step-in father may not know that Terri is too shy to speak in public, and that is why she looks at him to speak for her. New step-in parents haven't been around long enough to learn all a child's verbal and nonverbal cues.

Last night I was talking to a friend at church I hadn't seen in a long time. My son came up and tried to get my attention. "Just a minute, honey," I told him. "Don't interrupt."

I talked a few minutes more, and Tyler reached the end of his six-year-old attention span. He reached out for my chin and pulled my face toward him, talking all the while.

My friend laughed. "Does he do that often?" she asked.

"Only when he wants my full attention," I answered. "I don't think he thinks I'm listening unless I'm looking at him. I have to listen with my face."

Children need our full attention when they talk to us. We can do more than one thing at a time, so we often continue reading the paper or loading the dishwasher when our children talk. Children, however, are more single-minded than adults. We need to put down whatever we're doing and let them talk, especially when they need to talk about losses in their lives.

SOME FEELINGS CANNOT BE VERBALIZED

Young children, upset about family changes, may be unable to verbalize their feelings. Even infants and toddlers react with anger and confusion when their worlds change, and they cannot express themselves in words. Their frustration may surface in temper tantrums, crankiness, sleep disturbances, nightmares, bed-wetting, sleepwalking, or insomnia. If you notice these things, your child may be experiencing conflicting emotions that he cannot verbalize.

Our son, Tyler, was three when we moved from Virginia to Florida. I thought we all handled the move pretty well, but suddenly Tyler began to do two things that perplexed us. He had always clung to his favorite stuffed duck, but suddenly that duck and a McDonald's bucket never left his hands. For two months after the move he did not let either of those two things out of his grasp. We even had a family portrait taken during that time, complete with duck and bucket!

Harder to understand, our sweet and usually shy son began hitting every child in sight. We finally realized Tyler was frightened by the radical change in his life. He had a new house, a new church, and new neighbors. Even the weather was different. He couldn't verbalize his sense of loss, so he held on to two familiar items with all his might, and he released his anger and frustration the best way he knew—he struck out at every unthreatening person in his path.

Just as Tyler gradually accepted his new environment, your child will gradually accept the changes in her life. To encourage your young child's communication, you might try asking simple yes or no questions like:

"Do you feel angry because you have a new home?"

"Do you ever wish things were the way they used to be?"

"You know your mommy loves you, don't you?"

"Are you sad because you miss your brother?"

Many children react to change with a confusing array of emotions, and a thoughtful adult can help them sort through these conflicting emotions by asking careful questions. With older children, though, phrase your questions so the child has to think and give you more than a yes or no answer. Ask "why" questions when you're both in a comfortable mood; or, if that seems intimidating make a simple observation: "You were upset the other day. Want to talk about it?"

Communication skills should continue to be

sharpened long after the "breaking in" of the new family. At any stage of family adjustment, step-in parents should be careful not to make accusatory statements. If a step-in parent says, "You are so thoughtless! I've told you a hundred times not to leave the milk out on the counter," the child will feel thoughtless, dumb, and defensive. The next day he probably won't remember to put the milk away, and he may even forget on purpose because he's inwardly angry with the step-in parent for making him feel bad.

But if the parent begins by describing the child's behavior and then using an "I" statement to detail the parent's reaction, the child has a clearer sense of what he needs to do. It can also help to point out the logical consequence of the child's action or inaction. For instance, a parent could say, "When you forget to put the milk away, I feel frustrated and upset because I know the milk will spoil and we won't have milk tomorrow for our breakfast cereal. I also won't be able to make cookies for you tomorrow afternoon."

If Johnny wants cookies, he'll remember to put the milk away, and he'll be pleased with himself for remembering.

JOINT CUSTODY

No discussion of a child's sense of loss and loyalty would be complete without mentioning joint custody. I have two sets of friends who have divorced and arranged joint custody for their children. In one case, the girls spend every other night with Mom and every other night with Dad. In the other case, the boy spends three days with Mom and three days with Dad.

For many kids, life after divorce means two homes, two rooms, two sets of parents, two completely different ways of life. Is joint custody good for children?

First established in California in the late seventies, joint custody is now an established legal option in at least thirty-three states. In joint custody, both parents share legal and physical responsibility for their children. It seems a logical solution—both parents remain actively involved in the children's lives, and the children have a clear sense of who their parents are.

But does the constant shuffle between homes do anything to help a child feel secure?

The jury is still out. Dr. Judith Wallerstein, who is conducting a study on joint custody, has learned that children in joint custody whose parents are still angry with one another do not fare well. "The children become the shuttlecock in the war, subjected to the parents' threats, verbal abuse, and physical violence," she says. "This makes children feel very vulnerable and unprotected, and it is destructive to their mental health."[12]

"I don't think it is good for kids," a school counselor told me. "They belong in two places, and consequently, they really don't feel like they belong anywhere. That's very frustrating."

But children whose parents are at peace seem to enjoy at least certain aspects of joint custody. "The best part is you get to be with both your parents," says Maria, a ten-year-old from San Bernardino, California. "If I'm away from my mom for too long, I get upset. And if I didn't see my dad, I'd miss him because he's so big and nice, and he's the best tickler in the world."[13]

If you are involved as a step-in parent in a joint custody situation, cooperation will make life easier for everyone involved. If you are considering joint custody, the following questions may help.

Will you be living near the other parent? Children will forget important, irreplaceable things from time to time. If you must transfer the children frequently, it helps to live near the child's other parent.

Do you have an amicable relationship with the other parent? Children should not be exposed to angry confrontations each time they are picked up or dropped off. If you share the care of a child, you may need to speak to the other parent on a daily or weekly basis. Make sure you can speak peaceably.

Does your child handle change well? Some children do, and some don't. If your child likes sleeping in the same bed with the same toys every night, joint custody may not be a good arrangement for him.

Are you flexible? Children's needs change. As they progress to different schools, or during stages when they are learning developmental tasks such as toilet training, consistency is important. Custody arrangements should be reconsidered each year to make sure that the situation is best for all concerned.

Do both parents have the necessary space to accommodate the child?

Can you provide a full set of clothes and toys? You can't expect a child to pack all his belongings and move them every three or four days. It helps if he has all life's necessities in each household.

Are you willing to listen to your child? As children grow older, they want to have more control over their lives. If your teenage daughter, for instance, makes the marching band and Dad lives behind the football field, it may make more sense for her to spend weekdays in school with him. Listen to your children, and consider what they say.

At times all of us need reminding that children are people, too. In spite of our adult problems and concerns, our children need us to give them security, understanding, and at least some sense of power over their own lives. None of them want to feel "dealt out," as Erma Bombeck did. By understanding their sense of loyalty and loss, we can make things easier for our chosen kids.

NINE
Your Responsibilities and Rights

When we step in to parent a child, we should know our rights and responsibilities. If we do not, we may shortchange the child or face crushing disappointment when our expectations turn out to be false.

A step-in parent is in a unique situation. Morally, he may feel as responsible for the child as the biological parents—but legally, he may not have the right to make or enforce some of the decisions he thinks should be made. Legally, his authority over the child may be unclear or nonexistent; while morally, strong parental authority may be required.

When someone else's child enters your home and you agree, officially or informally, to act as a step-in parent for that child, what should you then expect?

AUTHORITY IN THE HOME

James H. Bray, an associate professor at Baylor College of Medicine in Houston, has studied stepfamilies for nearly seven years. He suggests that stepparents or step-in parents should function more like an aunt or baby-sitter at first. "Discipline should be left to the biological parent," he says.[1]

Mark Bruce Rosin, a step-in father, reported that he went very easy at first. "Sort of early on in the relationship I told them I didn't want to be their father. They already had a good relationship with their father. All I wanted to be was the male influence in the house, and that seemed to be agreeable."[2]

"With your stepchild, there is a degree of trust that just isn't there," Elise Berman told *Newsday*. "I can yell at my son, and he knows I still love him. With your stepchildren, there isn't that basic assumption to begin with. You have to earn it."[3]

It takes time to earn that love, and experts say it takes anywhere from two to seven years for a family to become firmly cemented together. And yet the home must continue functioning. Adults must guide children. Discipline must be enforced. Though it may require the wisdom of Solomon for a new step-in parent to take authority, I think we undercut the God-ordained authority of the elders if we do not allow a measure of authority to mothers and fathers and the people who step in for them. You should not allow a child to ignore you. You should expect your words to carry some weight. You are not a housekeeper, baby-sitter, or meal ticket.

While a child may be more inclined to listen to his or her biological parent, he or she still needs to hear and respect the position and authority of the step-in parent. If a child balks and claims, "I don't have to listen to you," the step-in parent should reply, "I am not your biological parent, true. But I am the man (or woman) of this house and you do have to follow house rules."

"I expect everyone in my house to obey the house rules," one step-in father told me. "It doesn't matter if they're my kids or my wife's kids or visitors. We have certain house rules, and when you're here, you're going to obey them."

DIFFERENT HOUSES, DIFFERENT STYLES

When people from different families come together, there are bound to be clashes. One family may love classical music—all the kids take violin and play in the symphony, and the sound system plays Beethoven while they barbecue on the deck. Other families are sports families—no Saturday is complete without playing in or watching a baseball, basketball, or football game.

But when a step-in parent arrives, kids who were used to Popsicles and ice cream may find salads on their plates instead. Kids who used to throw their dirty clothes on the floor and find them magically picked up may find that if they don't place their clothes in the hamper they face a raving lunatic. In some houses you eat after saying a blessing, in other houses you don't dare pick up a fork until the hard-working hostess has been seated. In much the same way that we adjust our behavior according to whether we are eating at McDonald's or the Swank Swan, kids will learn how to live by different rules in different houses—but the process may take a while.

Different houses reflect whether the family life-style is structured or unstructured. Step-in parents with relaxed, unstructured life-styles may find that children used to order and structure are uncomfortable and insecure in their home. More structured step-in parents raising free-wheeling kids may often hear complaints about things being "too strict."

Laura Barbash and her husband told *Newsday* about the frustration she feels when her husband's children come to visit. The children disregard the house rules she and her children have set up. They eat food in their rooms, neglect their chores, and talk on the phone for hours. "You know in his heart he's so scared of losing these kids that he can't see they're being destructive," she said of her husband. "But he can't use the same good judgment as he does with the kids who live in the house. So the resentments spill over to the other kids and onto us."[4]

When you act as a step-in parent, you may be faced with a child from a family life-style different from your own. "In the beginning, the fewer things you change, the better," Emily Visher says. "Choose a few rules that are most important to you, such as children must knock before entering your bedroom, and the dishwasher must be emptied each day, and let the rest go."[5]

DISCIPLINE: WHOSE AND HOW MUCH?

Discipline is often a source of tension for couples who are raising stepchildren. It is another area where couples often have unrealistic expectations. "Many times parents enter a relationship thinking they are going to enter fully into disciplining the stepchildren, deciding on family customs, and the like," says David Lambert. "If a biological parent has been raising a child alone he's probably been thinking, *Finally, I'm going to raise this child the way I think he should be raised.* He's been making decisions alone.

"But after a remarriage, suddenly there's someone else in the formula, too, someone that the biological parent may not fully trust to do what's best for the child. If he resists the efforts of his new spouse, the spouse feels like an outsider, or that she is not valued. The new spouse thinks, 'Hey, I live here, too,' and there's a big problem in the home."

For instance, if a woman has biological children and the husband immediately tries to fill a fatherlike role, she may resent his discipline of her children if she feels he is "coming down too hard" on them. But if she interferes in front of the children, she undercuts his authority, which adds stress to their marriage relationship.

To prevent these problems, parents should privately discuss the disciplinary measures they plan to take. Parents must present a united front, and each must be comfortable with the other's handling of the children. For help in setting up guidelines for discipline, read James Dobson's *Dare to Discipline* (Tyndale House Publishers).

Parents shouldn't be too hard on kids just to show who's in control. Educator Jay Kesler says a parent shouldn't always be commenting about a kid's hair, for instance. "A good rule of thumb to follow," he says, "is to ignore behavior which is not seriously detrimental to self or others. If misplaced hairs are not going to seriously offend anyone in particular, don't get caught up in making negative observations. Concentrate on positive reinforcement of good behavior. This kind of communication enhances self-esteem."[6]

For minor problems, set house rules and disciplinary measures that will stand no matter who dispenses the discipline. "You left the house without finishing your chores this morning," a parent might say. "You know that means you can't play outside this afternoon." Both parents must enforce house rules consistently.

For unruly kids who have a problem with obedience, draw up house rules at a family meeting. Explain the need for house rules and personal guidelines. Let the children know that we all live by rules that are in place for our safety and well-being. Allow the children to suggest appropriate disciplinary measures for when the rules are broken.

This "meeting of the minds" will help husbands and wives present a united front. Discipline should not be seen as coming "from him" or "from her," but "from Mom and Dad." When the husband and wife are comfortable with each other, they can usually work out their differences in front of the children. At no time, say Emily and John Visher, "does it work out for either children or adults to let the children approach each adult separately and 'divide and conquer.'"[7]

The Vishers caution against giving any sort of disciplinary action that affects the child when he is outside the household. If you ground a child for a week, for instance, so that he cannot take his visitation weekend with his biological parent, you've overstepped your boundaries and punished the biological parent as well as the child. You have no right to do that. It's better to ground the child for seven days while he's at *your* house.

Discipline may not be accepted until a relationship of mutual friendship and respect has been established. Usually if there is a biological parent in the household, he or she will enforce the discipline at first, but when that person is unavailable it is often necessary for the step-in parent to give a clear message to the children that he or she is acting as an authority figure and represents both adults.

"Kids have a lot of weapons in their arsenal when they want to be in control," says Dr. Philip Feldman. "They can be combative, hostile, demeaning, sly or sneaky. Often parents have allowed such behavior patterns to develop . . . because they feel guilty."

More damage is done by parental guilt than by neglect, says Feldman. Effective step-in parents set firm limits in love, not playing to the child's attempts to gain sympathy from or inflict guilt on the parents. Setting limits shows children that you care enough to demand certain kinds of behavior.[8]

"I spanked my stepkids just like I did my own kids," says Sherrie Williams. "They would have thought I didn't care about them if I didn't."

Setting limits is great, says author Paul Cullen. "But realize that those limits also are the walls your children will crash against to test you."[9]

One parent observed that there was more testing in

the early years. He called it the "breaking-in period" of "testing—pushing the stepparent out—doing things to make both parents angry—trying to push them apart. Now, after four and one-half years, there is recognition that there are plusses to be gained by my presence. There's also an awareness that I won't go away. More acceptance, less pushing."[10]

"My problem is that I have strict rules at my house and then my son visits his father where he's allowed to do anything," one mom told me. "What can I do?"

When your child spends considerable time in a household with vastly different house rules, it is especially important to teach not just rules, but the *principles* behind the rules. Don't just tell your son not to go to R-rated movies; instead, explain that what we put into our minds and hearts stays in our subconscious. Show him Philippians 4:8, where we are told to think on things that are true, noble, pure, right, lovely, admirable, excellent, or praiseworthy.

If you teach principles, your child will see the reasons behind the rules. He will learn to think and evaluate for himself. Ultimately, your child will be responsible for his own decisions, but until he is mature, enforce your house rules consistently with your actions and your words.

DETERMINE TO BE A PARENT

I appreciated Steve Newton's comment that when he married Elaine, he determined immediately to be a father to her two sons. Though the boys had a biological father, Steve knew he would not be happy in his own home unless he was fulfilling the role God intends for men to fill—that of the father and spiritual leader. Steve never intended to replace the boys' biological father; that would be impossible and undesirable. But in the Newton home, Steve is the father. Of that there is no question.

As they prepared for marriage, Steve approached his wife with an idea. "I wanted to adopt the boys," he says, "to be responsible for them. If anything happened to my wife, I didn't want the boys to go live with relatives, because I was going to pour myself into them. My future plans have been changed because of them, and I wanted the assurance they'd still belong to me if something happened to Elaine."

Steve was careful not to force the idea of adoption on the boys. "I made it clear that we wouldn't do it until they wanted it," he says. "After we had been married two years, they went to their mom and said, 'Let's do it,' so we did."

SHOULD YOU ADOPT THIS CHILD?

The question of whether to adopt children who live in your home is a sensitive one. My husband and I adopted children because it was the only way we could bring them into our home. Sometimes, when legally possible, foster parents adopt their foster children because the love is already there and they want to be legally recognized as a family.

Steve Newton adopted his wife's two boys because he wanted to safeguard his investment of time and love. Mel and Phyllis Atkins adopted their two grandsons to ensure the boys couldn't be removed from their home.

But for every couple who adopts their step-in children, there are many who don't choose to do so. Step-father Bob Williams did not adopt his wife's children. "I figured the girls would change their names when they married, anyway, so what difference would it make?" he asked. "We didn't need adoption to make us feel like a family."

"Adoption creates legal and financial obligations but not necessarily a relationship," says Paul Cullen. "A move to adoption may set up a challenge to the loyalty of a child toward a dead parent. A child of divorced parents may consider the move to adoption as a deep rejection by the natural parent, who is willing to give the child up."[11]

On the other hand, adoption can be a vote for security, proof that the family will stay together, and evidence that the child has been totally accepted by the step-in parent. Those who seek to adopt step-in children need expert legal advice from someone who is competent in stepfamily adoptions. Just remember that adoption doesn't necessarily bind people together; love does.

LEGAL RIGHTS OF STEP-IN PARENTS

Step-in parents have few legal rights unless they do adopt the children, but adoption is not possible unless the child's biological parents agree to relinquish their rights, the court declares the children abandoned, or the court terminates the parents' rights.

At present, step-in parents are not necessarily legally entitled to authorize emergency medical care or to examine a child's educational records. In a survey of Detroit-area hospitals, only a third would take care of a child brought into an emergency room by a stepparent (unless the situation was life threatening) without written authorization from the biological parent.[12] Some custodial stepparents have been unable even to pick up children at airports because they and the children have different last names.[13]

Biological parents have a strong advantage when custody arrangements are considered. For instance, even if you are named guardian of a child in the biological parent's will, and have acted as the child's parent for years, the surviving biological parent may get custody of the child.

Supporting a child financially and emotionally for years does not give a step-in parent legal rights. Even if they have disappeared from the scene, the biological parents retain greater legal rights to minors.

Grandparents raising grandchildren cannot assume their custody is guaranteed, either. "Permanent custody is complicated," a custodial grandparent told the *Los Angeles Times,* "but it's easier for the child, because they do not feel threatened." [14]

Mignon Scherer, another step-in grandparent, agrees. "There needs to be more emphasis on not giving the natural parent so many years to shape up and then get the child back," she says. "If a child is removed from the home, the parent is entitled to whatever is needed. But it isn't fair to the child to keep going back and forth like a yo-yo. Children need permanency. After a certain number of years, even if the parent makes some good changes, the current direction is not to return the child to the parent."[15]

At the state level, where family law is established, only six states have approved laws giving stepparents visitation rights to children after a second divorce. Appellate courts in eight other states—Pennsylvania, Connecticut, New Jersey, Oklahoma, Kentucky, Florida, Indiana, and Ohio—have awarded stepparents varying degrees of visitation rights.[16]

OTHERS HAVE RIGHTS, TOO

Because divorced mothers often choose to cut their children's ties with their paternal grandparents, grandparents in all fifty states now have the right to sue for visitation rights. But psychiatrist Andre Derdeyn questions whether it is wise to take family quarrels into such a public forum as a courtroom. He fears that "such legal initiatives by grandparents are likely only to add to the child's already excessive emotional turmoil if for no other reason than the initiation of such litigation being seen as a threat to the integrity and economy of the family by the parent or parents."[17]

Four psychologists from the University of Illinois and the University of Nebraska cautioned that broadening grandparents' rights may undermine the traditional emphasis on parents' rights and "engage families in new forms of intergenerational conflict (whether or not they are brought to the courtroom) in which children may be unintended victims."[18]

In other words, grandparents who are considering

legal action to sue for visitation rights should consider whether their efforts will damage an already-wounded family. Might it not be better to direct those energies to making peace with the estranged parent? Even in this situation, grandparents should take care to build bridges, not walls.

FINANCIAL CONSIDERATIONS

When you bring a new child into your home, you should sit down and examine your checkbook, savings account, and insurance policies. Some medical insurance policies cover stepchildren at no additional charge and others do not.[19] It is worth a call to your insurance company to find out if your step-in children are covered by your automobile and health insurance while they are living in your home. If you are bringing a teenage driver into the household, your rates are likely to increase.

If this child is to be a permanent member of your household, update your will or have one drawn up. Discuss with your spouse the provisions of your will, and if there are family heirlooms that you want specific children to have, clearly indicate what should go to whom in your will. Also be sure to name a guardian for your children. If you have remarried and want your spouse to raise your biological children, be sure to say so or the court may automatically award custody to the other biological parent.

When you step in as a parent, you and your spouse need to discuss long-range financial plans for this child. Are you going to pay for his or her college education?

For braces? For a car? For unusual medical expenses? If you are not, who is? A biological parent? A trust fund? The child welfare agency? Would it be better to have a separate account for this child's expenses? Although this may seem cold and calculating, it may prevent arguments and resentment in later years.

In general, stepparents have no legal obligation for the direct financial support of stepchildren, but some states are reconsidering this position. If a parent voluntarily takes on the support of a stepchild and the family divorces later, the stepparent is not legally required to continue supporting the child, because the voluntary assumption of a parent's role during the marriage, called *in loco parentis,* ended when the marriage ended.[20]

LEGAL RIGHTS OF FOSTER PARENTS

As I write this, Chicago is in an uproar over a seven-year-old girl called "Sarah." Sarah is a foster child who lived with Joseph and Marjorie Procopio from the time she was a newborn until she was five years old.

In 1989, Sarah's birth mother and her boyfriend convinced a Juvenile Court judge that they were off drugs and fit to be parents. Though psychiatrists testified that Sarah was better off with the Procopios and Sarah herself begged not to be taken from them, the little girl was returned to her birth mother.

The Procopios, who were not allowed even to visit Sarah at first, received help from *Chicago Tribune* columnist Bob Greene and the governor, Jim Edgar. In April 1991, a panel of the Illinois Appellate Court ruled that Sarah must be allowed to visit with the Procopios while she waits for a new custody hearing.[21]

Children like Sarah can remain in the foster-care system for years if their parents' rights have not been terminated. While they wait for these rights to be terminated or to be reunited with their families, no one, not even foster parents, can adopt the children.

Family therapists and other experts know the foster-care system needs a major overhaul. The ACLU brought a successful class-action suit in federal court on behalf of Washington, D.C.'s 2,200 foster children. Court documents showed that "temporary" placements often dragged on for years. One case cited was that of eleven-year-old Kevin, who was suicidal and admitted to a hospital at age eight. While there, he had climbed into a trash can and asked to be thrown away.[22]

Children need stable, loving homes, and the sooner their families can be stabilized or the children can be adopted, the better it is for the children. In Florida, where I live, state law requires that once a judge has decided a child in foster care is dependent, the biological parents have eighteen months to prove to the Department of Health and Rehabilitative Services that they are capable of taking the child back. If they are not, government authorities must find adoptive parents. It sounds like a good law, but children actually stay in foster care from twenty-nine to forty-eight months.

THE RIGHTS AND REWARDS OF FOSTER PARENTS

The foster-care system has damaged some children, but how many more would be damaged if it did not exist? While some situations and abuses are dreadful, there are also success stories. Some Christian parents hesitate to become involved in foster care because they do not personally agree with certain aspects of the system (the ban on corporal punishment, for example), but their influence is desperately needed.

What rights do foster parents have? Not many. Marilee Kastle, who has been a foster parent for four years, was told she does have the right to adopt her foster children if the biological parents' rights are relinquished or terminated. But not all foster parents have that assurance. "The social workers combined the training for foster and adoptive parents, so we went through both," she says. "And we were told we had first right of refusal should the children be available for adoption. But the two children I have now are part of a sibling group of five, and they'd probably offer me all five children should the situation arise. Our adoption of them would depend on if government authorities are willing to split the sibling group."

Foster parents receive financial help, but for dedicated foster parents, the amount isn't enough to cover the expenses of raising a child. "My little boy's birthday is this week, and we're throwing him a big party and buying him a bicycle," Marilee says. "Of course none of that is covered in the monthly amount we receive as foster parents. Once I got a clothing allowance to buy school clothes for the kids, but the next year we were told there was no money for that. The kids do get a Medicaid card to cover medical expenses, but you have to find a doctor and dentist who will accept it."

Foster parents have the right to have children

removed from their homes. Marilee exercised that right once. "I had a little girl who had been sexually abused, and I wasn't trained to deal with that," she says. "She really needed to be in a therapeutic home, but a child has to fail in three foster homes before they can be placed in a therapeutic home. But I called the government authorities and said, 'I can't deal with this,' so they placed her in a therapeutic home."

Fortunately for the children, Marilee says that the government authorities do not go out of their way to move children around. "If the child is happy in the home and the foster parents are happy, the child will stay in place until he is moved by the court," she says. "But if they wanted to move a child for some reason, a foster parent has no say in what the court does."

Marilee's foster kids call her Mommy. "They tell you not to encourage it," she says, "but I've had these two kids since they were small. The older foster kids I've had called me by my first name, but I'm really all these two have ever known."

If Marilee's foster children were returned to their biological parents next week, she would be allowed to visit only if the biological parents allowed it. Otherwise, her time with the children would be ended.

Such a conclusion is emotionally painful. So why does Marilee continue to open her home to children who will be there only temporarily? "We have learned not to take anything for granted," she says. "Our hearts go out to all foster children who seem to wander aimlessly through the system and never have a permanent place to live.

"Our children have taught us humility in that they

have nothing, but continue to give and receive love. My foster son Andrew would do absolutely anything for me—he even asks to help in the kitchen. They ask us who made the clouds and sky, and the simplicity of their questions brings us back to the simple things in life."

TEN
When Changes Come

It is a secret both in nature and state, that it is
easier to change many things than one.
—Francis Bacon, *Of Regimen of Health*

Elizabeth Ryberg works as a medical assistant in
pediatric oncology at the North Carolina Children's
Brenner's Hospital in Winston-Salem. She and her
husband, Ed, love kids. That's why they volunteered
to be foster parents.

"We wanted to fill our household with as many kids
as we could," she told me once. "Ed has always loved
children, and so have I. I don't believe God makes
mistakes when he makes children."

Before their first biological child was a year old, the
Rybergs opened their home to a fourteen-year-old boy
named Joe. Joe lived down the street in a house that
rocked with life. There were eight or nine kids at home
as well as Joe's alcoholic father. Joe would walk by the
Rybergs' house when he got off the school bus, and if
Elizabeth was out in the yard he'd stop and talk. If

things were bad when Joe got home, he'd go back to the Rybergs' house and stay until his daddy either left or went to bed. As long as his mother knew where he was, the Rybergs didn't mind having Joe around. In fact, when they moved to another neighborhood, Joe got permission from his parents and moved with them. He stayed with the Rybergs for over a year until they had to move out of state.

Their love for children led the Rybergs to investigate foster care, and they took in one child whom they later adopted. "She was diagnosed as retarded, and they told us she would never walk or talk," Elizabeth recalls. "But now she's a straight-*A* student. The Lord really blessed us with her. She's a delight."

The Rybergs took in another child, a three-day-old, mixed-race baby girl, whom they called Holly Beth. Holly Beth's biological parents had relinquished their parental rights. "She was simply beautiful," Elizabeth recalls. "She had olive skin, brown eyes, soft curly hair, and even as a baby her bright personality just shone."

The Rybergs kept Holly Beth for ten months before they even heard from a social worker. Later they were told her file had been temporarily "lost in the shuffle." The Rybergs let the Department of Social Services know they wanted to adopt Holly. All that had to be done was update the Rybergs' file, since they had already adopted through the department.

When Holly was thirteen months old, the Department of Social Services called and said they were going to send Holly to a white couple in New York. They gave three reasons, none of which made any practical sense to Elizabeth. First, they said, there were more interracial marriages in New York and Holly would be more comfortable—but the Rybergs had already started a growing support group for couples with mixed-race children in their area. Second, the department said the other couple had already adopted a mixed-race child only one month older than Holly. Finally, they were concerned because Elizabeth had once had cancer.

The Rybergs couldn't accept any of those reasons. Hadn't they just adopted a child through the department? Hadn't they both passed their physicals? What difference did it make that Holly would have a sibling one month older? They felt the trauma of moving Holly would greatly outweigh any imagined benefits of a move to New York.

The social worker said the department's decision was final, but Elizabeth began to look around for legal help. Meanwhile, the couple from New York flew down and visited with Holly one afternoon. They arranged to pick her up the next morning and spend the day with her. Elizabeth had to admit that at least they were doing their best to make Holly feel comfortable with them.

But the next morning the couple didn't show up; the social workers did. As Elizabeth slipped the last button on Holly's coat into place, one social worker grabbed the baby and the other scooped up her diaper bag. Out the door they went, as quickly as they could, while Holly screamed in terror and confusion.

Elizabeth leaned against the door, weak-kneed. She spoke aloud: "No child ever came to my house kicking and screaming, and no child will ever again leave kicking and screaming." She went to her phone and got help.

Elizabeth found a lawyer who flew through the system and got a restraining order so that Holly couldn't be taken away from the Rybergs the next day. "We only wanted what was in Holly's best interests," says Elizabeth, "but I hadn't seen anything to indicate the Department of Social Services felt the same way."

The next morning the social workers appeared at her door to get Holly. Elizabeth told them Holly wasn't going with them, and one of them asked, "Do you realize how destructive you're being?" Elizabeth thought only of how destructive they had been yesterday to the well-being of the child she had grown to love. Elizabeth quietly and politely told them about the restraining order, and they finally left.

"We were ready to give Holly up if it was in her best interest," says Elizabeth, "but the way they were handling it, we couldn't see that it was. To our surprise, a judge at the hearing gave us custody while we were waiting for the superior court hearing."

The Rybergs waited for over a year, and during that time they moved to another county. Finally, on a hot summer day, they received word that the judge had ruled against them.

Social services in the county where they had lived issued a pick-up order for Holly through the sheriff's department, but it wasn't valid in the county where the Rybergs were now living. So Holly Beth stayed with them, still a part of the family.

Finally, when Holly was three years old, the Rybergs

were summoned to appear in court in their former county of residence. They had to go, and they had to take Holly with them. But they were comforted because they had the right to testify at the hearing, so Elizabeth and Ed wrote out their testimonies. "We documented everything and thought of every detail, and did our utmost to give Holly the best chance of staying in the only home she had ever known," Elizabeth says.

They drove in silence, their plans laid like a battle strategy. Elizabeth and Holly would go to a holding room in the courthouse to wait for their lawyer. Ed would go into the hearing and give their testimony. They were sure the judge would rule in their favor.

But when the elevator doors opened on the fourth floor where the courtroom was located, there were no holding rooms. There was only an outside corridor, and waiting there were a battery of social workers and the lawyer for Social Services. "We have an order to pick her up," the lawyer said, reaching for Holly's hand.

"No," Elizabeth said, pulling her away. "We've come to testify before the judge." Elizabeth picked Holly up and held her tightly.

The deputy tried to take her from Elizabeth's arms; and Elizabeth felt her strength sap. She couldn't hold on to Holly Beth. Holly didn't cry, but she reached out and called, "Mommy." Elizabeth saw her, heard her, and fainted.

Elizabeth's daughter told her what happened next. The lawyer, deputies, and social workers turned and left. Ed came into the hall and saw Elizabeth on the floor. He ran for Holly, but got to the elevator as the doors were closing. That was the last time he saw her.

The Rybergs' lawyer hadn't even arrived. Acting on the authority of the old pick-up order, the social workers in effect canceled the summons to the courtroom. The Rybergs never had a chance to testify and give their side of the story.

Later that afternoon their lawyer showed their testimony to the judge, who said he would have ruled in favor of the Rybergs. But with Holly gone, the previous ruling against them was allowed to stand.

Holly Beth was the Rybergs' last foster child.

"That was our last experience with foster care," Elizabeth says. "When the opportunity came up for me to work with terminally ill children, I took it because I know what it's like to lose a child. I have no idea where Holly is, and I just have to put her in the Lord's hands."

IF THE ONLY CONSISTENCY IN YOUR HOUSE IS CHANGE

I'm telling Elizabeth Ryberg's story not because I want to criticize the foster-care system but because every step-in parent must expect change and the losses and rewards it can bring. Elizabeth Ryberg went through a rough time, but because of that experience she took a job caring for children with cancer. She has instituted a program for those children that has made a tremendous difference in hundreds of lives. As he always does, our God brought good out of loss.

Regardless of the reasons, just or unjust, change comes to all families. Most of us find change uncomfortable, unpleasant, or downright distressing, but change helps us grow as individuals and as families. Change keeps us from being stagnant in our spiritual lives.

Change can come:

- when a parent becomes ill and can no longer care for the children
- when the parent with whom the children live decides the children would be "better off" in the other parent's family
- when children, particularly teenagers, decide they want to live in the other family
- when a single parent feels overburdened or angry and sends the children to the other parent, suitcase in hand
- when a remarried parent finds that having a "home" again reawakens the desire to see more of his or her children
- when a parent is unable to care properly for the children
- when foster children return to their biological parents
- when the court decides to move foster children or change custody rights
- when a parent dies

MANY ROLES TO PLAY

Stephanie Archer has been through many family forms. She was married when she undertook raising two infant granddaughters. She then went through a divorce. "I was a single grandparent raising two little girls," she says. "Through faith and obedience I went through a rough ordeal, but God had a plan."

Sixteen months ago Stephanie married Harold Archer, and they share custody of Harold's fourteen-year-old daughter with his ex-wife. Stephanie has filled the roles of grandparent, stepparent, single parent, and biological parent. At fifty, she knows the future can still bring change.

SOMETIMES CHILDREN COME

> I recently moved and switched from living with my stepfather and mother to living with my stepmother and father. I feel totally comfortable with my stepmother as I've known her since I was three years old. We have our share of problems, but she treats me like her son and I equally treat her as a mother. We get along fine because of the respect that we show each other. —Peter, age seventeen

Susan Donim, a professor in the Boston area, married George when his children were ten, twelve, and thirteen. "When we married, there was never any idea that a child would move in with us," she recalls. "Their mother was extremely jealous of her role, and no one was inclined to challenge her."

But four years later, fourteen-year-old Ted moved in with Susan and George. "He was in the midst of a full-scale adolescent rebellion, attempting to define his manhood in the face of his mother and two older sisters in a household with no men," Susan recalls. "His mother couldn't stand it anymore, he couldn't stand it anymore, and everyone agreed that he would come to live with his father—and, incidentally, with me."

"It almost destroyed my marriage," she says. "Bringing a stepchild into a family encourages tremendous conflicts between the natural parent and the stepparent: jealousies, resentments, confusions over different methods of child rearing that haven't had years to sort themselves out, problems with the ex-husband or ex-wife."[1]

Bringing a stepchild into the family does *not* have to destroy your marriage. Donim explains in her article in the *Boston Globe* magazine that she was ill-equipped to handle raising a teenage son. She had no clearly defined role and no authority. She was not prepared to be a mother, only an older friend. She attacked her husband and "drove him under cover" because she resented carrying the burden for "a child who wasn't even mine."

These attitudes are typical, but they are not inescapable. If you will commit to loving this "instant" child, you will find the appropriate role for a step-in parent. Many of us adoptive parents like to tell our children that their biological parents gave them life, but we are giving them a *home*. You can do the same thing. While the child is with you, you are providing a home, and you need the authority to be the mother or father of that home.

Cathy and Ty Ortega married with five children between them. Ty's three, Keith, Tommy, and Natasha, lived with his ex-wife, and he promised Cathy that she would not be raising his children. "I had explained that I didn't think I would be very good at raising someone else's children," Cathy says. "In fact, our marriage was out of the question as far as I was concerned

if we would be raising the children—for their sakes."
Ty agreed from the beginning that Cathy's two sons,
Daryl and Carl, would live in their home.

Within their first year of marriage, however, Keith
arrived at Cathy and Ty's home after being suspended
from school. When Tommy got into trouble and was
suspended from school too, his mother called Ty and
Cathy to say that he was on an airplane and they
should pick him up at the airport in thirty minutes.

"Needless to say, I was not a happy camper," Cathy
says. "Natasha came within three weeks of Tommy,
and I drew the line! She was impossible, and we had
Tommy to deal with at the time."

Natasha returned to her mother, but she came back
to the Ortega's home within a year. So Cathy Ortega,
who didn't want to raise Ty's children, had them all
full-time.

"The difference is obvious to me, to Ty, and to both
sets of children," Cathy says. "I think it is a natural difference: no matter what my children do, I love them
anyway. It is much easier to tolerate deficiencies, bad
habits, and mistakes in my natural children. With Ty's
children, I have to work at it, and I don't always succeed. I am sure Ty feels the same way.

"I care very much for Ty's kids. My love for them is
an extension of my love for Ty and something that has
grown through the years. I have a relationship with
them that has been cultivated with time, prayers, and
mostly God. With natural children, though, it is all
there without any work at all."

"Also, though we have been through lots of changes
and rough times, we've tried to maintain consistency

in certain areas. Our rules are strict but firm. We've never labled the kids—I always introduced all the kids as my sons and daughters. So does Ty. I think that subconsciously it made a difference to them, and it was a form of commitment on my part that they were 'my children,' too. In the beginning the kids did use the word 'step,' but they don't now and haven't in the last seven or eight years."

RECOGNIZING THE ITCH TO SWITCH

In our work with young people, my husband and I have talked to several kids from divorced and broken homes whose first reaction to trouble at home is "I'll go live with my dad" or "I'm moving in with Mom. She'll take me." Is it wise to allow kids to switch homes?

There is no clear-cut answer. Each couple and each family must evaluate their situation independently. If the child is merely going through a simple angry spell or rebellion over a specific incident, the itch to switch probably will pass quickly. But if there is a pattern of discontent and disruption, might a switch be in order?

Before allowing a child to move from (or into) your home, consider the following:

Are you (or the other parent) willing and able to accept the child? Some parents may be unable to provide financially for the child, or living arrangements may make it impossible for them to assume custody. Many kids, however, will see a biological parent's inability to receive them as rejection.

If you allow this move, will the child see it as a successful power play? Children should be told that if they

are allowed to move, it will be because *you* have
thought about it and agreed. Kids cannot simply
threaten to move as emotional blackmail.

*Does the child understand that things will not be per-
fect in the other household, either?* Remind the child
that he or she will have to undergo the "breaking in"
phase all over again in the other household. The child
may have to settle in again at a new school, in a new
neighborhood, with new friends, at a new church, etc.
It's not easy to make a change.

Can you agree upon a set time for this move? Moving
a child in anger at a moment's notice and for "forever"
does little to help his self-esteem or your frazzled
nerves. A move should be accomplished carefully,
with thought, and should be done at a convenient time
for all. It also might be a good idea to suggest that any
move last for a minimum time period of, say, six
weeks, six months, or a year, so the child doesn't
bounce right back to where he or she began.

*Would the child benefit from being with his or her
same-sex parent?* Teenage boys and girls may benefit
from living with the parent of the same sex, but this
is a judgment call, especially if there are other male/
female figures in both households.

*What effect will this move have on the household he
or she is leaving?* No man is an island, and the child's
absence will have an effect. How will it affect his or
her biological parent? Will he or she feel like a failure
if a biological son or daughter leaves? Will another
step-in parent feel guilty? Will the other children
mourn the loss of a brother or sister? Carefully discuss with your child the effects leaving will have on

other family members, friends, educational and career goals, and spiritual life.

HOW TO ADJUST WHEN A CHILD MOVES IN

"It is difficult to have a new person or persons move into your 'space,'" say Emily and John Visher, "and it is difficult to be the 'new' person or people joining a preexisting group." The Vishers suggest that, when possible, step-in families move into larger, neutral quarters. Such a move is natural when a couple marries again, but if you are receiving one or more children after your marriage, you might give them a room alone or to themselves, at least for a short period.

If you do not have children of your own, the Vishers suggest that you take a course on child rearing or read good books on the subject. Talk to another step-in parent in a similar situation and remember that everyone will feel a little strange at first. At first it will seem like having company in the house, but that awkward feeling will fade with time.

If the incoming child is your or your spouse's biological child, accept the fact that one of you will naturally be closer to the child than the other. It will take time for you to share equal footing, and you and your spouse will feel differently toward the child.

It is important that everyone in the family be as flexible as possible. It will take time to adjust.

When new children arrive in the household, there is usually a "honeymoon" period where everything is perfect. After the honeymoon, though, comes the time of testing. The child will test two things: the consistency of the house rules and your commitment to his or her care.

I've always believed in firm boundaries for children. At our house we have set bedtimes and well-defined expectations. I believe that children do better when they have clear ideas about what is expected of them.

The new child in your family will poke and prod to see just how far he or she can go. Don't be surprised if sixteen-year-old Susie stays out past her curfew or if nine-year-old Tommy wanders three blocks too far from your home. They want to see if you mean what you say, and if the house rules—and the consequences of breaking them—are consistent.

The children also want to know just how far they can go before you will snap and send them back. They may not want to go back, but they want to test your level of commitment. If you say you love them, be sure that love will be tested. If you say, "You're welcome here," that welcome will be tried. All you have to do is grit your teeth and hold on.

Children who move in temporarily, though, often cause havoc. Ann Patchett writes of the summers when her four stepbrothers and sisters came to stay:

> My mother and stepfather were attentive to us, raising us to be the kind of children they wanted to have: neat, quiet, polite. But every May an unknown element was dumped into the beaker, and the family blew apart. Suddenly nobody was playing by the rules anymore: wet towels were left on chairs and on the floor, dishes were left in the sink, there was noise and fighting, and

somebody was always leaving the front door open—behavior that was perfectly acceptable in their house.

In our normal life we had freedoms and were respected as individuals. In the summer we were made to line up according to age and count off whenever we went anywhere. I went from being Ann to being Number Four. It was like we were trapped in those early scenes from *The Sound of Music,* before Maria comes and explains to the coldhearted captain that children are people, too.

My stepbrothers and sisters opened up my world; they made me realize there were other ways of doing things, new ways of thinking and behaving. There was a second-story balcony that overlooked the living room, and they soon discovered it was possible to stand on the banister and jump fifteen feet down onto the sofa. After watching in horror for about five minutes, I was up and over the railing myself. It was an incredible feeling, doing something dangerous just for the sake of doing it.[2]

SOMETIMES CHILDREN GO

Janet Bailey's thirteen-year-old daughter flew to visit her father and stepmother. Twelve hours before she was scheduled to come home, she called her mother and said she wanted to live with her father permanently. "I knew she was changing," Janet wrote in an article in *Family Forum*. "Acceptance by her peers was extremely important to her, and her fathercould provide her with material things I could not."

Janet was overwhelmed by her daughter's decision, but she clung to the promise of Isaiah 41:10: "So do not fear, for I am with you; do not be dismayed, for I am your God. I will strengthen you and help you; I will uphold you with my righteous right hand."

A few months later, Janet's daughter came back home to live. "During the time Carolyn was living with her dad," Janet writes, "I had to keep praying to God for His will to be done. I had to totally relinquish Carolyn into His care. I didn't know what was best for her, living with me or with her dad. But I knew God did, and I trusted His decision for her life."[3]

When change takes a child from your home, not only do you ache for the missing child, but others in your family notice the gap, too. Joe and Marilyn Dahlman are foster parents and have four biological children. When their latest foster child, Michael, was reunited with his family and left their care, they noticed strange behavior from their four-year-old son, Justin. He was aggressive and disobedient, completely unlike himself.

Finally Marilyn had a clue. "Are you afraid you'll go away, too?" she asked. Justin nodded.

Marilyn smiled. "Honey, you're a belly baby. You came out of Mommy's tummy, and this is your home. I am your mommy."

It isn't easy to see children go, but once the initial pain of departing has subsided, we ought to be able to say we have done the best we could for the time God brought us together.

LOVING LONG-DISTANCE: WHEN A CHILD IS AWAY

When the child you love leaves your home—whether
it is a biological child whose custody has been awarded
to someone else, a foster child, a grandchild, or a niece
or nephew—it may be hard to maintain emotional closeness with him or her. You may quietly bite your lip when
the new custodial parent calls to remind you of the
child's shoe size or suggests that the last gift you sent
was inappropriate. It's not easy to think that someone
else knows more than you about the child you love.

How can you remain an important presence in this
child's life? For starters, take advantage of the telephone, and don't be put off if the child is involved in
something else when you call. Through the immediacy
of a telephone call, you can be present for instant, wonderful happenings and special celebrations. You can
call on special days just to say you care or "I'm thinking
about you today." Just don't be hostile to the adults in
the other household or allow the child to use your
advice as ammunition against the parents he or she
lives with.

Don't expect the child to drop everything she's doing
to have a heart-to-heart talk on the phone. When you
call, you can't know beforehand if she has chosen that
moment to pout in her room or have a crying jag. You
might call during her favorite television show or during
mealtime. Children aren't the most considerate crea-
tures on earth, and they may not truly appreciate the
effort you are making to stay in touch.

But hang in there. Strive for consistency. Keep those
calls and letters and care packages coming. Be a presence, not a rare surprise.

Learn the names of the people closest to this child you want to influence: his teacher, pastor, coach, principal, and neighbors. Drop these people an occasional note or give them a call to ask how he is doing or to express your appreciation for the role they are playing in your child's life.[4]

Encourage your parents and your siblings to maintain contact with this child. Send snapshots of yourself. If you take a trip or a vacation, send pictures so he will know what you're doing. Let him know what you do, and who you are, and tell him about your dreams.

Finally, pray for the child you love. We play an active role in the lives of the people for whom we pray, so set aside time each day to pray specifically for the child who is away from you. Make a prayer list and tape it inside your car or above the kitchen sink or on the refrigerator. Pray for him, and assure him of your prayers.

You have a unique place in the child's heart. You can forfeit your special place or you can use it to give him good influences and positive instruction. The choice is yours.

HAVING A NEW BABY: "YOURS AND MINE" BECOMES "OURS"

What happens when step-in parents have a baby? How does the new baby affect the other children in the household?

Esther Birenzweig, who runs a stepparent program in Toronto, says a new child can bring a family closer together. "The new child gives each member a common element," she says. However, she believes that a mutual child strengthens bonds in a family only if a strong relationship exists between the couple and their stepchildren and if the parents are prepared to treat all children equally. Some parents may spend more time with and give more privileges to their biological children, which will cause tension and friction in the home.

Birenzweig suggests that couples who decide to have a mutual child help their other children feel more comfortable by including them in preparations for and care of the new baby. Parents also should encourage the children to talk about their feelings toward the new baby.[5]

Most step-in mothers welcome a chance to love one child unconditionally and freely, the way a mother loves her biological child. A step-in mother who has been struggling to raise stepchildren, for example, may inwardly rejoice that at last she will freely feel the love she's worked so hard to maintain with her stepchildren. This child, at least, will call her "Mommy" without hesitation.

With the arrival of a baby, step-in mothers may feel more confident. Their sense of power increases, and as a result, they may feel free to "loosen up" and allow the other children more independence. If an insecure step-in mother's role is fulfilled and settled with the birth of her biological baby, she doesn't have to prove anything with the other children in the home. As a result, everyone wins.

Having a mutual child, however, does not always draw a family closer together. Sometimes, particularly when an ex-spouse is involved with the other children, a new baby can cause jealousy, friction, and anger.

Dr. Anne-Marie Ambert, a York University sociology professor, says that a noncustodial parent may find his or her biological children alienated by the idea or presence of a new baby.[6] Even ex-spouses can feel threatened and jealous when a new baby is on the way.

When Sally and Mitch Michaelson married, Sally stepped in as mother to Mitch's two children, Stacy, seven, and Collin, four. "I feel like we bonded right away," she says. "I've always loved children, and I didn't care whose they were. I thought it just didn't matter."

When Sally became pregnant with her first child, Stacy began to spend more time on the phone with her biological mother. "She kept reminding Stacy that they were not related to me by blood," Sally recalls. "She told them I would never love them like my own. This went on for three years."

Sally was overjoyed about her pregnancy and thought her stepchildren would be thrilled, too. "I talked with Stacy and Collin about how big the baby was, and they'd feel the baby kick through my tummy. When the baby was born, I brought home presents for each of the kids, you know, from the baby, so they wouldn't feel left out. But while I was in the hospital, their natural mother called and wanted them to come visit for the first time in over a year.

"When I came home from the hospital with the baby, there was a lot of pain that hadn't been there before. Their mother had told them the baby wasn't really their sister, and my mother wasn't really their grandmother, stuff like that. As exciting as my baby's birth had been, I came home to devastation.

"From that time forward, things went downhill. I'd be breast-feeding the baby, and Stacy would walk in and say, 'That's gross. Why are you doing that?' She was constantly on me about everything, putting me down, but I think there was a time when she really loved me. They were just overcome with insecurity, and their birth mother complicated things."

When Stacy was thirteen, she asked Mitch and Sally if she could go live with her mother. "We had custody, and we agonized over the decision, but Mitch decided to let her do it," Sally recalls. "Once we told her she could go, she started working on her brother. Although they weren't even very close, he soon came to us and said he wanted to go, too. That was devastating to both of us."

Mitch and Sally let the children go, not knowing what else to do. "We knew the environment was not good with their mother, at least not what we wanted, but we felt we had to let them learn on their own or we would lose them forever," Sally says.

"A lot of people have told me you can never love stepchildren like your own," Sally says, "but I don't agree. But the children have to be willing to have the relationship, too. I think my stepchildren do love me, and in time, they're going to come back around and see that I did provide a great home for them, but they have to be older before they can appreciate that. I have a lot to give, but that doesn't mean the kids are going to accept it. And when tough times come, step-in mothers can take a lot of blame."

In other situations, a baby can cement a family together. With the impending arrival of the new child, the other kids in the family see with suddenly clarity that it truly isn't "us" against "them" anymore. The family has become a "we." And together, "we" are having a baby.

Bob and Sherrie Williams recall how it was when their daughter, Gaylyn, was born. "Suddenly we were a family," Sherrie says. "Everyone loved Gaylyn. We had ten kids, and we loved it. We still have that sense of family togetherness."

"The new baby is the one person in the family to whom everyone is biologically related," says Dr. Katherine Baker, a social worker with a private practice in Washington, D.C. "The arrival of the new baby makes a statement both to the outside world and to the inside world of the remarried family about the family's commitment to a future as a stable child-rearing unit."[7]

In the ideal situation, remarried couples should discuss the idea of a mutual child before they marry. If one person wants another child and the other doesn't, the friction can tear a marriage apart. One person may have already raised a child and not want to return to diapers and doctor's visits and high chairs and late-night feedings. The other person may desperately want a biological child, a personal link to the family's posterity. These issues are important and should be discussed.

Grandparents may find their role changing with the birth of a baby in a blended family. When the children involved were stepgrandchildren, the grandparents had a certain level of involvement, but if and when biological grandchildren are introduced, the grandparents may be surprised at their desire to increase their involvement in the family. Grandparents should be careful, however, not to slight other children in the family by favoring a new baby.

The birth of a new baby may even increase the parents' stake in the family. Whereas one parent may have been reluctant to engage in discipline or structuring of the family, now that he or she has a direct stake in the family, his or her role may change. "They now have a chance to set goals together for a child from the beginning of a child's life," writes Paul Cullen. "They have the new challenge of working out a joint system of discipline. And the shared child will affect their time alone."[8]

Yes, new babies bring change and challenges. But change is the turning of the kaleidoscope that keeps family life an ever-swirling blend of colors and patterns. Even though change is sometimes painful, it brings its own beauty to life.

ELEVEN
Too Angry for Words

I don't like my stepfather at all because he treats me and my older brother like dirt and treats his real kids wonderful. It makes me sick! —Angela, age twelve and a half

"I hate you! You're not my real mom!"

"I hate you! You're not my real dad and I don't have to do what you say!"

"I hate my mom. . . ."

"I hate my dad. . . ."

"I hate myself. . . ."

Hate and anger. Step-in parents shouldn't be surprised when these emotions surface.

"In the early years of my marriage, I resented it," says Jim Flotho, a step-in father to three girls. "I felt I had to prove myself as a provider and father, but the 'I hate you' made me feel like I wasn't doing a good job."[1]

SaraKay Smullens, a family therapist, calls anger "the killer of second marriages."[2]

HURT FEELINGS

How does anger begin? With hurt. And children of divorce, children removed from their homes, or children who have been abandoned hurt plenty. They ache. In my work with young people, I've seen kids so torn by loyalties to Mom and Dad or so hurt by the continuing battles between ex-spouses that suicide seems the only way out of their pain. At age thirteen and fourteen, they've given up hope.

Hurt can also arise from little things. Each child reacts differently when his home is sifted or rearranged, and petty jealousies can erupt into hurt feelings.

Yesterday my husband took the kids to McDonald's for a Happy Meal. As they pulled out of the parking lot, Taryn erupted in angry tears because she didn't get a toy in her lunch bag and Tyler did. She didn't care about the toy, but her sense of justice had been violated. It just wasn't fair that her brother got something and she didn't.

When you are faced with an angry child, look for the feeling underneath the anger. The child could be feeling scared, torn, or jealous. "The child may be scared that they won't see their other parent as much, or the child may be feeling disloyal to the other parent or worried that the stepparent is trying to take the parent's place," Emily Visher says.[3] Use the angry confrontation as an opportunity to give whatever reassurances the child needs.

Cathy Ortega recalls the time when her husband's children arrived in their home. "The kids were confused, frustrated, and neglected," she says. "I know they were and still are bitter about the divorce. Natasha and Kevin still use it as an excuse for their problems. I'm sure it *was* the basis for many of their problems at first. Their life was not easy after the divorce, and had we known the way things would ultimately end, we would have taken them all in the beginning."

The child you step in to parent may feel cheated. He may sense that something is missing from his life. This may be particularly true if one or both of his biological parents have disappeared or do not wish to contact him. Your child may wonder if somehow she is unwanted or unlovable. She may feel that she doesn't deserve love or a happy home, and so she may misbehave to make reality agree with her perception of herself.

OTHER STRESSES AGGRAVATE THE SITUATION

The number one source of stress in remarriage is the way step-in parents handle their new roles.[4] Not only are you tackling the hardest job on earth, parenting, but you're doing it with a child you don't know very well. You may feel about as secure as a camel on ice skates.

Children can make a stressful situation worse by allying themselves with one parent. Foster children can cling to one parent, bringing hurt and frustration to the other parent. Stepchildren can ally themselves with their biological parent, virtually ignoring the step-in parent. Children have an uncanny ability to turn the tables on a couple and play Mom and Dad off one another.

Cathy Ortega says she felt like an ogre when Ty's kids came to live with them. "All Ty's kids came to us angry," Cathy recalls. "Their mother was not giving them a home, and they weren't being nurtured in any way. They were constantly in trouble to get attention, and since we had to start our relationship in a mode of discipline, there was a lot of anger. I tried to give love and discipline, but I know I did not handle it well at first because I was busy being bitter and angry that I got the kids in the first place. Also at that time my mom died, and my dad had a heart attack. It was a very rough time in our lives."

ANGER CAN BE MISPLACED

If you hear "I hate you," realize that the anger may be misplaced. "You tend to be angry at the person you can best stand to lose," says Emily Visher. "The child may be angry at the biological parent, but it's safer to be angry at the stepparent."[5]

"There's a lot of anger, and often it is misplaced," says Philip Feldman, a Philadelphia psychiatrist and marriage counselor. "The child who is angry at his parents for the family breakup punishes the stepparent, and the angry ex-spouse may try to sabotage the stepparent's relationship with the child."

Ideally, says Feldman, a step-in parent will accept a child's pain and give his anger time to heal without getting upset by it, "but that is rarely what happens. Instead a child is pressured to produce instant feelings of love for the new family members."[6]

Step-in parents should realize that anger also can come from a loss of control. "The children didn't have control over the divorce, or the death, or the remarriage, or where they live," says Visher. Allow your children to have control over as many aspects of their lives as possible. Let them choose what to wear and what to eat for breakfast. Allow them to decide what the family will do on an occasional "family night" together.

Counselor Dottie Hartman says that many children who seem chronically depressed may be dealing with repressed anger. "One of the impotencies of childhood," she says, "is that expressing anger is not approved by anyone and tolerated by only a few." She remembers that her own parents once let her quietly sing to herself, "I don't like Mom or Dad," over and over again. When a child does express such anger, Hartman believes parents should say, "I understand that you're feeling angry, and that's okay. But when you decide I'm okay again, will you share that with me, too? I'll leave you now, but I won't go too far."

ANGRY EX-SPOUSES AND NONCUSTODIAL PARENTS

Often the symbol of trouble between step-in parents and biological parents is the telephone. For years Margaret Roth and her husband's ex-wife, Cindy, were tethered to the telephone, and Margaret says they "weren't trading recipes for meat loaf."

Margaret's husband wasn't speaking to his ex-wife, so "any arrangements we made with the kids were made between Cindy and I," Margaret recalls. "The kids were too young to do it. And Cindy wouldn't talk to Dick any more than Dick wanted to talk to her. I was squashed in the middle."[7]

The relationship you establish with the children's

noncustodial biological parent, if such a relationship can exist, will influence your family's life-style. Your holidays, traditions, birthdays, free time, weddings, vacations, and weekends could be affected by whether you have let go of any anger that might be directed toward the other parent.

"There can be a lot of antagonism and anger with the ex-spouse, and it can get displaced on the present marriage," says Phyllis Roth, a clinical social worker. "Whether the fights have to do with maintenance payments, child support, visiting schedules or who has the kids for the holidays, often they'll nitpick to cross every T and dot every I, and all it does is keep them in contact. Even though the [marriage] relationship has been put aside legally, they're still involved in the fighting and the screaming and the demanding. They just can't let it finish."[8]

If yours is a remarriage and you are the new spouse, you may be drawn into the fray. New spouses can be dragged in to referee the arguments, or you may be unwittingly worsening things by encouraging your spouse to dwell on the offenses, real or imagined, of the ex-spouse.

"The hottest relationships are usually the mother-stepmother issue," says Massachusetts family therapist Florence Meyer. "The second wife can feel that the first wife is drawing an incredible amount of attention and energy from her husband. And even though it's hostile energy, it's still time and focus away from the new wife."[9]

Claire Berman advises adults involved in a child's life to let go of their anger. She quotes Patricia

Greschner-Nedry, a California mother: "One of the things I came to realize is that being angry at my former husband wasn't changing things, but it was taking up a lot of time."[10]

"It's very freeing not to spend your life angry and hostile," says Emily Visher. "It allows you to move on to other things."[11]

Cathy Ortega says that anger isn't something you just "get over" and never have to battle again. "The one time I felt insecure and a tad bitter," she says, "was not long ago when our son Tommy got married. It's hard to be mother during the hard times and then move over for the biological mother during the happy times when she wants to be the center of attention. Of course, in the Lord, all things are possible, and we got through it. I know I will feel the same way when Natasha gets married, because we will plan the wedding and do all the work and her biological mother will show up for the event and want to be center stage as usual. I will deal with it then, too, but I don't have to like it."

Anita used to show her anger toward her ex-husband by grilling her girls about what they did every minute of the weekend with their father. Finally she decided she was putting the girls in the middle of her squabbles with her ex. "It changed when I saw his wife took good care of them and did a lot of things with them," she says. "I want them to like their father—I even want them to love him."[12]

Anger and fear are companions. Time eases the passing of anger, and security helps wipe out fear. Margaret Roth recalls how she felt when she and her husband passed their eleventh anniversary: "They were married eleven years," she says, speaking of her husband and his first wife. "And when we were married eleven years, I started counting: Eleven years and one week, eleven years and two weeks. Now that it's reached a full twelve years, I've reached a new point: I'm not that kid, I'm not that girl, I'm not the second wife or the new wife. I'm the wife."[13]

WHEN YOU AND YOUR SPOUSE BATTLE

Pearl Prilik has noted that most conflicts between a step-in parenting team spring from five areas: unequal treatment of children in the family, one spouse's lack of involvement in child care, unrealistic expectations, the intrusion of the biological parent(s), and a loss of romance in the marriage.[14]

Just as the little foxes spoil the vineyard, little things can destroy the peace in your home and marriage. Squabbles among the children, visitation schedules, the awkwardness of a child who moves in later than the others, issues of privacy, and the clash of parenting styles all bring diverse and sometimes volatile emotions onto a field of battle.

If you've let any of these situations develop so that you've acted or reacted wrongly to your spouse, Philip Feldman advises you to "get back on track by discussing the kids as 'our family' instead of 'yours.'. . . Instead of saying 'your child' lies, cheats or steals, smokes pot or whatever else you may suspect, try saying, 'I feel uptight when . . .' or 'I don't know what to do when . . .' Tell each other how you feel about the current behavior, not the child's past upbringing."[15]

CHILDREN FEEL ANGER

Whether the ex-spouses are battling each other openly or silently, the resulting tension inevitably spills over into the new marriage and ultimately onto the kids. "Kids who do the worst in remarriage are usually a product of a marital conflict that never ended," says therapist Larry Taub. "Most times, the exes are locked into 'victory is just around the corner' in their old marital conflict, and they won't give it up. The fight is worth more than anything, including their child's life."[16]

When children are helpless to do anything about their anger or the tension in the home, they look for a way to escape. Too often, that means running away. Robert Sweet of the Office of Juvenile Justice and Delinquency Prevention notes that almost all runaways are teenagers. Even more significant, "disproportionately, these teenagers are running from families with stepparents and live-in boyfriends or girlfriends. . . . Runaways reflect the disintegration of the American family."[17]

An Australian study found that "adolescents from disrupted families reported higher levels of general health problems, were more neurotic, less extroverted, had poorer perceptions of their bodies, were more impulsive, and had more negative views of their school performance."[18]

"Well, that's not my kid," you may think. "He's adapted very well to our new family." But older kids are often adept at hiding their true feelings. If your child seems to be handling his or her new situation well, don't assume that he or she really is unless you've had a chance to sit down and share some heartfelt questions and answers. One teenage girl told me, "I have to be strong and act like everything's okay for my dad's sake. I can't hurt, but it does hurt, a lot."

Teenagers are profoundly affected by changes in their families, and they are at an age when they can express this anger and unhappiness in dangerous ways. They may begin to use drugs or drive dangerously or hang around with reckless kids. Girls may seek love outside the home, and reason that a premarital physical relationship will not only fit the bill, but "get back" at Mom or Dad, too.

"In the early stages of remarriage, both sons and daughters are hostile, sulking, negativistic, and angry not only at their stepfather but at their mother," says Mavis Hetherington, a University of Virginia psychologist who has studied children in families with stepfathers. "They're mad as heck at their mother for remarrying."[19]

Why is this? It probably has much to do with the emotional closeness children develop with their mothers or fathers during the time of single parenting. Often the parents are depressed or stressed from the divorce and the demands of single-parenting, and children assume adult roles to care for and protect their parents. When the parents remarry, giving up that nurturing role is not easy.

ANGRY TEENAGERS

Angry teenagers can be especially difficult to deal with because their usual way of expressing anger is through unacceptable behavior. How do you handle a teenager gone wild? Every child spells trouble sometimes. But some children, especially in their adolescent years, can turn trouble into a pain-filled way of life for their families. Violence, profanity, crimes, substance abuse, sexual activity, refusing to abide by house rules—such irresponsible acts are in a different league from the usual parental challenges.

"These home-shaking disappointments make you understand why the word rebellion happens to contain the words 'rebel' and 'lion,'" writes R.A. "Buddy" Scott in his book, *Relief for Hurting Parents*. "Living with an out-of-control teenager can be like living with a lion on the rampage!"[20]

Scott directs a Christian counseling agency in Lake Jackson, Texas, that provides hundreds of hurting families with practical guidance and a spiritual perspective. I spoke with him by telephone about angry teenagers. "God understands how hurting parents feel," Scott declares. "God lost his kids . . . and no one can say he didn't raise them right."

What is the difference between big-time angry rebellion and normal adolescent dissension? Scott explained: "There are small indicators and huge indicators. If you look at a mountain range you can usually see foothills in the foreground and huge, jagged mountains in the background. The 'foothills' are the small indicators—a child's withdrawal from the family, criticism of the traditional values of the family, and friendship with kids of lesser moral character. Also included among these 'foothills' would be friends who call and won't give a full name, the rejection of the youth group at church, and fudging on curfew. In the foothills, a child is beginning to edge into wrong things, but he does it slowly and keeps his activities hidden.

"In the jagged 'mountains,' though, teenagers don't come home at night, a girl skips school, a boy comes home drunk, a best friend is arrested for dealing drugs. Or a parent finds an incriminating note about sexual involvement or involvement with drugs.

"The typical reaction of adults to tyrannical teens is shock and trauma," says Scott. "They have tried to love the teenager unconditionally through crisis after crisis, and they ask, 'This is our reward for trying faithfully?' Theirs is a different kind of hurt—it's worse than being fired after you've done your absolute best."

As a step-in parent, if you have done your best to guide the child in your care, you are doing a decent job. "The misbehaviors of children do not necessarily indicate we are failures," Scott says. "We deserve respect. If we are seeking to heal children and save them from damaging themselves morally, spiritually, emotionally, socially, and physically, we are *decent parents.*"

Too often step-in parents react badly when a child rebels. Scott has seen adults lose their tempers, slap or hit teenagers, and even curse them. That approach will not work, Scott cautions.

Step-in parents should not react in such ways, "If you *reject* kids, you will *eject* them toward the wrong crowd, and the wrong crowd will be happy to reel them in," says Scott. "We need to reject kids' wrong behavior but reassure them of our love and trust. We have to let kids know things can get better. We need to maintain our Christian witness. This gives kids a decent environment for improvement."

How should step-in parents discipline angry teenagers? Aren't they too old for spanking? And what good is grounding a kid when he has a VCR, telephone, stocked refrigerator, and stereophonic sound?

When disciplining, step-in parents should first decide whether the problem was the result of flagrant rebellion or ordinary teenage antics. "Do not," Scott says, "make giant hassles of normal teenage problems."

If the problem was normal teenage mischief, be patient. If it was an act of willful wrongdoing, discuss it with your spouse and resolve to respond in unity. "Resolve to be shepherding parents, not vengeful, attacking, or punishing," says Scott. Discipline should be done with the desire to teach, not to belittle, obtain revenge, or make the child miserable.

When deciding what to do, consider what would be the natural consequence of the teenager's actions. If it is possible, allow the child to experience the pain of his wrong choices. But before acting, ask yourself, "Will this heal?" If your response will not lead to healing, change it.

Scott suggests that step-in parents tell their angry teenager, "We love you and we know you have good qualities even though you have made a mistake. But because you have chosen to teach us that you can't be trusted (lack self-control, etc.), you have chosen for us to respond by keeping you at home (or by not buying that jacket, etc.). Here's how you can teach us to trust you again in the future, and here are the positive rewards for your success: (name the conditions and rewards.)" Listen to the teenager's response.[21]

While the uncomfortable consequences are taking place, be supportive of your child. Remind him or her that it will be over soon. With such an attitude, step-in parents allow their children to see that discipline is something children bring on themselves, and even though parents have to act, their promise to love is firm.

GRANDPARENTS GET ANGRY, TOO

At a weekly therapy support session of Grandparents as Parents, eleven grandmothers gathered to discuss the stresses of raising their grandchildren. Fifty-three-year-old Bobbie Brantley, who is raising a four-year-old granddaughter, said, "You give up your hopes and dreams—even of just going back to school, or just going walking.

"I had about two months without anyone being in the house," Brantley said, reminding the group that all six of her children are grown. "I had changed everything around. Now I had to change things again. I had to get diapers, a baby bed, baby food, a stroller. All that had been dumped. I hadn't planned on raising any more."

Alta Edwards is caring for three grandchildren: an eleven-year-old boy, a seven-year-old girl, and a seven-year-old boy. She talks about the challenges of rearing kids in a different world than the one she knew: "My seven-year-old grandson knows. Hey, this kid knows whether or not they're smoking dope. He knows when they're selling it."

V'ann Corliss raised four children as a single parent. "When the last one was grown and left, I said, 'Hallelujah.' It was tough, but we made it and it's over." Then the parents of her grandson began having problems, and the boy came to her house and asked, "Grandma, can I live with you?"

Sharon Scott, who is forty, cares for two grandsons. "My three-year-old was born with heroin in his body," she says. "How do I cope? Just barely. I worry a lot that I'm not doing right by them. Always as parents, we think we can do better. I'm real concerned that they turn out to be better than their mother."

The grandmothers express concerns about homework (they don't know how to do it), overwork, foul language, and wanting to reach out to their grandchildren but not quite knowing how.

Seventy-five-year-old Patricia Phelps is raising her nine-year-old grandson. Her health isn't what it could be, and her grandson is headstrong, she says. "It's sometimes rough, but I could never let him go to a foster home. I had other plans for my life, but I think God gives us things to do."[22]

A study by the University of Louisville School of Medicine found that the major therapeutic task for grandparents raising grandchildren is resolving anger toward the parent of the children.[23] Other frustrations for grandparents include the need for love, anxiety about the future, manipulation by the parents, changing mores, the suppression and denial of the grandparents' own needs, dealing with resistance and denial, and the emotional demands of the "job." The study also suggested that the clearer the custody status in favor of permanent custody for the grandparent, the less anxiety, uncertainty, and conflict with the natural parent existed.[24]

WHAT TO DO ABOUT ANGER

"We've been brought up to believe that nice people don't get angry," says Paul Cullen. "But anger can be very positive. Anger at the child custody system prompted [one father] to join with other noncustodial parents to push for legislation to protect their rights to see their children."[25]

"In your anger do not sin," the Bible tells us in Ephesians 4:26 and Psalm 4:4. It is okay to be angry as long as that anger doesn't lead us to sin. You can judge whether your anger is sinful or not by examining two areas: what makes you angry and what anger makes you.

What makes you angry? Jesus was angry when he threw the moneychangers out of the temple. They had distorted the meaning and the purpose of worship, and I'm convinced the world didn't see the anger of a wimpy fisherman that day in the temple! Jesus was mightily angry because he was defending the work of God.

Anger that comes from wounded pride, though, is wrong. If we are angry when our selfish desires are thwarted, our anger is sin. That sinful anger can be our undoing. "Anger resides in the lap of fools," says Ecclesiastes 7:9. Unless we want to be foolish, we need to dump that kind of anger out of our laps!

But people hurt through divorce, death, abandonment, or jealousy often feel an anger too deep to be wished away and too intense to be "talked out." If not dealt with, this anger festers and evolves into bitterness. And bitterness, which is not God's will for a Christian, has dire physical and spiritual consequences.

What does anger make you? Sick. Anger and bitterness can lead to disease. Ulcerative colitis, peptic ulcers, heart attacks, arthritis, strokes, migraines, and high blood pressure are just a few diseases aggravated by the stress anger puts on the human body. The Bible tells us that bitterness affects bone marrow, the "factory" that produces blood cells:

"When I kept silent, my bones wasted away through my groaning all day long" (Psalm 32:3).

"A cheerful heart is good medicine, but a crushed spirit dries up the bones" (Proverbs 17:22).

"A heart at peace gives life to the body, but envy rots the bones" (Proverbs 14:30).

If we harbor hate and anger in our hearts, we cannot love God as we ought to. "If anyone says, 'I love God,' yet hates his brother, he is a liar. For anyone who does not love his brother, whom he has seen, cannot love God, whom he has not seen" (1 John 4:20).

We need to freely forgive those who have hurt us, because if we cannot, we cannot freely ask God to forgive us. "For if you forgive men when they sin against you, your heavenly Father will also forgive you. But if you do not forgive men their sins, your Father will not forgive your sins" (Matthew 6:14-15).

Anger is enslaving. S. I. McMillen, author of *None of These Diseases,* writes: "I have found that the moment I start hating a man, I become his slave. I can't enjoy my work anymore because he even controls my thoughts. I can't escape his tyrannical grasp on my mind."[26]

Anyone can be angry, but there may be no group of angrier people than those brought together in the nontraditional family web. Secular experts on family life will tell you that anger is to be expected; it's normal, it's natural, and you can live with it comfortably. But as Christians, we are to "sin not" in our anger, and the best way to make sure our anger does not dissolve into bitterness and cling to our souls is to get rid of it.

SWEEPING ANGER OUT THE DOOR

How do you rid yourself of anger? The most direct avenue to erasing anger is forgiveness. Forgive the offending party, even though your forgiveness will cost you something: maybe money, maybe your pride, maybe some time with your child.

Another route to unloading anger is to see the other person's perspective. Are you angry with your child's biological parent? Try feeling as she feels. Try to understand the insecurity that may be a huge part of her life. Realize the pressures she is under.

Think for a moment about your step-in child's noncustodial parent. What is he or she feeling? She may fear losing her children's love and loyalty. He may fear that his child will be shut out of his former spouse's new marriage. She may be overwhelmed by personal or financial pressures. He may have no outside emotional support. And certainly noncustodial parents resent it when an ex-spouse does something for the new spouse or family that he or she never did for the first.

"How does a noncustodial father get past his bitterness?" a Florida father wrote to a *USA Today* advice column. "I've been told I can spend five days a month with my daughter!

"My ex-wife has a boyfriend now. And my son is with him more than with me.

"My ex always takes our kids nice places, and I can't compete."[27]

Anger between two people can be defused if you see the situation as a problem to solve together, not an adversarial jousting match. "Let's work this out," you could say. "I'm willing to give a little if you can meet me halfway." State your concerns clearly and listen to the other person's point of view. In the long term, you and your family will come out ahead if you rid yourself of anger and its ills. Remember, most of life's lessons are caught, not taught, and your children will watch how you handle anger.

Andrea Peters told me what her sons, Doug and Steve, learned from watching the quiet lessons taught by a step-in father:

"Doug was very angry when his biological father left home," Andrea recalls. "For fifteen years he had taught Doug that certain things were wrong, and then he left home to go do all those things. Doug had been very proud of his dad, but then his dad let him down.

"Doug was a strong Christian, though, and he kept witnessing to his dad. It worried him that his dad, who had never touched alcohol, was drinking and becoming an alcoholic. His dad, who had been a preacher, was now using foul language, being dishonest, not caring for his family, and living with a girlfriend. Doug, on the other hand, had to help support me, his brother, and sister as well as finishing his last two years of high school.

"Doug was eighteen when I met Chuck. We dated for a year and a half, which gave the children time to get to know Chuck, and Doug liked Chuck and wasn't against our getting married. But he felt insecure about living with us. He was willing to pay room and board and didn't want to be a burden. He kept saying he would get a place of his own. We knew he was afraid and insecure about the right thing to do, so we encouraged him to live with us and pay fifty dollars a month room and board.

"Doug came to respect Chuck and then to love him as a real friend. Chuck helped Doug when his car broke down. Chuck loaned Doug a car, and then Chuck arranged to get a ride to work. Doug has *never* forgotten that."

The family equation changed when Andrea's other son, Steve, moved into the household. Steve had been living with his father, and when he moved in with Chuck and Andrea, more than the usual problems arose. "Doug and Steve used to fight in the kitchen when they were both getting ready for work. Chuck would referee, but he never lost his cool or his Christian testimony. Doug watched, too, as Chuck accepted the responsibility of supporting Steve.

"Steve had been involved in drugs, he smoked, and when he came to us he had an infected toe that cost Chuck over five hundred dollars in medical bills. He had a lot of needs, but Chuck never once got angry about taking on a stepson with so many problems.

Steve was angry about *everything,* but Chuck helped him find a job and an apartment when the time came and paid for some serious surgery he required. Steve was unhappy with his life and felt lonely. He lashed out at everyone.

"When it came time for the boys to be married, their father wouldn't help with any expenses, so Chuck paid for everything that the father of the groom usually pays for. Now both boys are extremely grateful to him and have a deep respect and love for him.

"Today both boys and their families are committed to the Lord. I believe it is because they witnessed how God turned bad into good. They saw how I had to depend on the Lord to meet my needs, but God was faithful in every way. They were also healed because Chuck ministered to them with loving patience, sacrificial giving, and a true testimony of Jesus Christ 'living in him.'"

TWELVE
The Rewards of Loving Someone Else's Child

The best thing about living with a stepparent is the relationship between us. It's a bond that will never be broken. I would tell other stepparents to treat your son or daughter with respect and love because what you give to them will always come back to you. As time passes, they won't really think of you as a stepparent. —Kevin, age eighteen

The best thing about living with a stepfather is the guidance and instruction he gives you. — Chad, age fifteen

An associate of mine, a man involved in Christian ministry, told me a little about the struggles a parent faces when a marriage fails. Through the pain and effort, he learned that God's love and light still shine through.

"Through the most painful trials of my life, I've seen some surprising changes begin to happen in my heart," he wrote in a recent editorial. "Call them encounters with grace. I have found that those empty spaces that I had held in contempt are also doors and windows. They give entrance into my life to Christ, the wounded Healer, the One who told Paul, 'My strength is made perfect in weakness.'

"Last year, against all my wishes and prayers, my marriage ended. . . . Since then, [my children and I] have tried to find new ways to have a family; the one we had hoped for just isn't going to happen. So much remains to be understood and accepted. But I can tell you this: in our times of deepest need, we have felt God's tenderness."[1]

THE KEY TO SUCCESS

Many books on family life, though full of good advice, leave out the only key to success in loving someone else's child. The key is simple: *Love that child the way God wants you to love him or her.* That's all. If we can put aside the past and our petty hang-ups and love the children God brings into our lives as he wants us to, we will be successful as God measures success.

God's ideal of family love and fidelity is at odds with the world's philosophy. The world says, "Look out for yourself. You've got rights, you know!" God says those who love best love sacrificially, not considering themselves.

Judy Thomas of Seattle, Washington, is raising her son and two stepdaughters. She says it was her faith that helped her adjust as a step-in parent. "You need to develop a good relationship with the Lord to face the severe challenges of dealing with someone else's children," she says. "You have to be willing to bend, or it's fatal. Perhaps it is impossible to do that without a strong relationship with the Lord."[2]

"Too often," says Jerrie Goewey, "we don't like our behavior, our spouse's behavior, our kids' behavior. We think, 'Who needs this stuff?' But faith reminds us that 'I promised.' It opens our minds to options. It's not magic. If we don't have faith, though, it's too easy to decide not to make the effort to save a marriage that's in difficult straits."[3]

God can help in any difficult situation you may face as a step-in parent. But God's way of helping is not to remove us from trouble, it is to equip us to go through the struggle with an extra helping of heavenly strength and grace.

So when you seek God's help, be ready for change. God will begin to work, first in you, then in your situation.

STRONGER AS THE YEARS GO BY

Cathy Ortega says that her marriage to Ty would not have lasted without God. "I found the Lord about eighteen months into our marriage, and although we were headed down the same destructive path as our previous marriages, we realized divorce was not an alternative anymore. So we were stuck with each other. It was at that point that I got down on my knees and asked God to put our marriage back together again. God was faithful to answer, and our marriage has grown stronger as the years go by.

"Once I found the Lord, our family became a matter of constant work and prayer, prayer and work. Ty and I seldom argued except concerning the kids, and it was a struggle to deal with four troubled children.

"I know without any doubt that our family would not have remained a family without Jesus in our lives. It was only through prayer and perseverance that we are still a family today. And the church helped. Two of my younger children were raised in church and had the benefit of good youth programs.

"But we are survivors because of God. I am sure we would have failed outside of the Lord. If I could offer advice to another step-in parent, it would be this: don't give up—pray. Don't be hasty—pray. No matter how tough times were, we never had a situation that we couldn't handle with God."

INVISIBLE INVESTMENT

You may feel that your investment of money and time and love into a child's life is useless. Perhaps you are working with an indifferent child or an overtly hostile one. But consider your investment "invisible." It may not become visible for years, but you must have faith that it will.

Your godly influence and testimony *will* affect the children in your care. The Bible tells us that Jehoshaphat was blessed by God because "in his early years he walked in the ways his father David had followed" (2 Chronicles 17:3). Uzziah became king of Israel at age sixteen, and "he did what was right in the eyes of the Lord, just as his father Amaziah had done"

(2 Chronicles 26:4). And Paul was proud of the young Timothy, who was influenced by his mother and grandmother: "I have been reminded of your sincere faith, which first lived in your grandmother Lois and in your mother Eunice and, I am persuaded, now lives in you also" (2 Timothy 1:5).

These people watched their fathers and mothers and grandmothers walk in the way of the Lord. When they were mature, they followed in that way.

In your role as a step-in parent, whether or not you have custody of the child and whether or not you feel your love and concern are returned, you are an example and testimony to the power of God in your life. Strive to keep that testimony strong, and seek God's will in all that you do. Then you will lay a firm foundation, the "invisible investment" that may prove to be a bedrock for your child's future.

DELAYED BLESSINGS

God, unlike us, is not interested in instant gratification. He brings blessings in his own time, when we have learned what he wants us to learn: patience, forbearance, trust, obedience, and steadfastness. The Israelites marched for seven long, hot days around Jericho before the walls fell. The Messiah foretold in Genesis 3:15 did not appear for millennia. Jesus did not instantly heal the demon-possessed daughter of the Canaanite woman who cried out for him (Matthew 15:22-28). And Peter was kept in prison until God sent his angel to release him (Acts 12:5-7).

We cannot expect God to wave a magic wand and

solve our problems. We go through troubles, not because God is mean or vindictive, but because he wants us to learn lessons about his strength, his supply, and his steadfast love.

THE REWARDS OF STEP-IN PARENTS

What are the rewards of step-in parenting? Is loving someone else's child worth your time and tears? Writing in *Redbook,* Betty Rex explains why she loves other people's children as a foster mother:

> Since 1960, my husband and I have taken in more than ninety foster children—some for only a few weeks, some for several years. Why do we do it? Certainly not for the money—because the amount we receive is only a reimbursement for money spent, not a salary.
>
> But the rewards are many and varied. Last Christmas, for example, a young man showed up at our door, searching for a piece of his past. He had left our care twenty-five years earlier, at four months of age. The agency had given him our names along with the names of his natural parents. I still had the hospital infant-identification bracelet he had worn on his tiny wrist when he came to us immediately after his birth, the recipe for his baby formula and some baby pictures— all of which I gave to him.
>
> When people ask us how we can bear to let our foster children go, I think of Michael [a child I had for several years]. What these people must understand is that a parent's role with *any* child is to

help that child grow up strong and independent so that he can eventually leave. Our life has been made richer for having known Michael. Part of him will always remain with us and, I hope, we will always be a part of him.[4]

The stability and godly influence of a Christian foster family may be the most important thing a child ever experiences. Likewise, stepfamilies, even with their problems, can give children unexpected benefits.

UNEXPECTED BENEFITS FOR FAMILIES

John Santrock, a psychologist at the University of Texas, has studied stepchildren ages six to eleven and concluded that although boys living in families without fathers are a little slow in their mental development, the addition of a stepfather seems to close the gap.[5]

Even the complexity of a stepfamily can be beneficial to children. "For example," says Glen Clingempeel, "a stepchild could have up to eight sets of grandparents and stepaunts and uncles. That's more people with diverse personalities and styles and backgrounds and so there are more sources of social and cognitive stimulation for kids. In the long run, kids in stepfamilies could be developing more effective ways of dealing with a greater variety of people."[6]

Children with step-in parents usually have multiple role models. They will observe different parenting techniques and will have more models from which to choose when *they* are parents someday.

Families with step-in parents learn that it pays to be

flexible. Researchers Nick Stinnett and John DeFrain found that strong families have problems like anyone else, but they face crises with determination and flexibility. They focus on the positive; they draw upon their spiritual resources; and they adapt and change when necessary. They know that the family, with all its problems, is still the place for development and comfort, regeneration and revitalization. As one woman told them, "I put love into my family as an investment in their future, my future, our future. It's the best investment I can make."[7]

As a step-in parent, you may be offering a child additional siblings. On some days, you may wonder if that is really a blessing, but it's very likely that all the children in your household will benefit from the added opportunities for play, conversation, understanding, and sacrifice.

Nicholas Zill, executive director of Child Trends, says, "I have cautious optimism for stepfamilies. There's evidence so far that the majority of stepfamilies are able to adjust well."

What we consider the ideal family—a mom, a dad, and a couple of kids—hasn't always been the normal family. In the nineteenth century, nearly one-fourth of all children under the age of eighteen saw one of their parents die, says Dr. Frank Furstenberg, a sociologist. Remarriage and stepparenting have been common for a long time.

In the 1960s however, divorce began to overtake death as the major reason families separated. Today almost half of all children are not living with both their parents.

Stepfamilies "are as good as other families in terms of their ability to adapt to problems and to change," says psychologist James Bray. "They're just less connected [than intact families]."[8]

"The reality is that there are a lot of positive benefits for stepfamilies," says Thomas Seibt, a marriage and family therapist in Los Angeles. "I think kids can come out of a stepfamily with the opportunity for a lot better model of what a happy and good family can be like."

"THEY'LL COME AROUND"

Bob and Sherrie Williams have been through every challenge a stepfamily can offer. When they married and combined their nine children, one of Bob's boys wanted to live with them in order to "spy" for his mother. Bob said no. Soon two of Bob's daughters left to live with their mother, too.

Sherrie's first husband had died, so her children had had to grieve and had decided that Bob wasn't going to take his place. Sherrie had to learn to handle telephone harassment, because Bob's first wife was alive (and kicking!).

Bob was used to doing laundry at two in the morning. Sherrie was used to being mother and father to her kids. Together, they had to learn how to divide family chores and find new roles. They each had to pull back and give the other room to function as a vital part of the parenting team.

Sherrie says that although the kids fought like brothers and sisters at home, they "stuck together like glue" at school. But it wasn't like "The Brady Bunch." Sherrie's girls were sometimes defiant at first, and Bob often felt "on the out." After the passing of time, though, they learned to respect his firmness.

Interestingly enough, Sherrie's first husband's mother, Grandma Patterson, is still in the family. Bob "adopted" her, as did all the kids. She's the grandma of the clan, accompanying them to church on Sundays and coming over for the weekly Saturday family get-togethers. Since both Bob's and Sherrie's parents are dead, she's the only grandma the kids have known.

Today Bob and Sherrie's family includes Grandma Patterson, ten kids, and eighteen grandchildren. "There are a lot more challenges in our family," Sherrie says, "but our family isn't really different from any family on the street."

Sherrie has this advice for step-in parents: "Trust God. You can't do it on your own. Love them like your own, and treat 'em that way. Don't ever say, 'I'll send you home to your mother,' because if you've agreed to take these kids on, they're yours. We never called the kids 'stepchildren,' and we each disciplined the kids freely and fairly."

Bob adds, "Accept them where they are because they came from a different environment and a differ-ent set of parents. Work with them patiently, and they'll come around."

LASTING IMPRESSIONS

Many noncustodial step-in parents are concerned because they have so little time with the children. *How can I impart Christian values to this child when I see him for only a few weeks of the year?* a stepparent or grandparent may wonder. *How can I even get to know him?*

"Since children tend to resist concerted efforts by the adults to instill family ideals during each visit," say John and Emily Visher, "it is comforting to parents to learn that the examples of behavior and relationships *simply observed* in the household can affect choices made by all the children later in their lives."[9]

There is probably at least one person from your childhood who, by some word or action, made an impression on your life. Recently I picked up a special issue of *Newsweek* and read Lynda Barry's story, "Guardian Neighbor." Mrs. Yvonne Taylor was the special lady in Lynda's childhood neighborhood. "I knew right away there was something different about her," writes Lynda. "It was a look she had when you talked to her that we had hardly ever seen on an adult. She looked like she was actually paying attention."

One day Lynda sneaked over to Mrs. Taylor's house at dawn. Mr. Taylor, in his bathrobe, opened the door, and Lynda was escorted into the kitchen:

> I'll never forget that morning, sitting at their table eating eggs and toast, watching them talk to each other and smile. How Mr. Taylor made a joke and Mrs. Taylor laughed. How she put her hand on his shoulder as she poured coffee and how he leaned his face down to kiss it. And that was all I needed to see. I only needed to see it once to be able to believe for the rest of my life that happiness between two people can exist.

And I remember Sammy walking in and crawling up onto his father's lap, leaning his head into his dad's green coveralls like doing that was the most ordinary thing in the world. Even if it wasn't happening in my house, I knew that just being near it counted for something. When I got back home my mother told me she was ready to wring my neck. She couldn't figure out why in the world I kept going over there to bother those people.[10]

Just being near it counted for something. I only needed to see it once to be able to believe for the rest of my life that happiness between two people can exist. How well Lynda Barry says it!

Whether you love someone else's child for an hour or a lifetime, you can make a positive difference. There are challenges to be faced, but the rewards are great. Don't give up. Pray. And confidently step in to help the child who needs you.

RULES FOR CONFIDENT STEP-IN PARENTS

1. *Be proud of the role you are assuming.*
2. *Be realistic. Check all rosy expectations at the door.*
3. *Love your spouse.*
4. *Be flexible.*
5. *Respect yourself so the children will be free to respect you.*
6. *Remember that you are not a replacement. You are an original, crafted and equipped by God to meet whatever comes your way.*
7. *Take time—to adjust, to listen, to pray, to play.*
8. *Let go of destructive anger.*
9. *Reach out for help when you need it.*
10. *Watch for invisible blessings.*

RESOURCES FOR THOSE WHO LOVE SOMEONE ELSE'S CHILD

Stepping Stones is a unique Christian seminar ministry for stepparents taught by Wayne and Sharon Pribbernow of Muskegon, Michigan. "We are stepparents and we had so many problems in the beginning," Sharon says. "Finally I realized there were just some things we'd have to deal with that other families don't deal with: visitation, the ex-husband and the ex-wife, strained finances, the past. Once we stopped trying to deny this, we were well on our way."

For information on how the Pribbernows can conduct a one-day seminar in your area, write "Stepping Stones," 31 West Grand Avenue, Muskegon, MI 49441, or call (616) 722-7837.

Strengthening Families is a curriculum kit that offers in-depth group studies for stepfamilies. Authored by Elizabeth Einstein and Linda Albert, the series is published by the American Guidance Series, Circle Plains, MN 55044-1796.

The Stepfamily Association of America, 602 East Joppa Road, Baltimore, MD 21204, may have information you can use. Their telephone number is (301) 823-7570.

In your local newspaper you may find meetings of support groups such as Grandparents as Parents or Grandparents Raising Grandchildren. Your local library may know of such a group in your area.

Foster parents have a range of services available to them including training, counseling, financial assistance, and medical coverage for foster children in the home. "We've even provided prom dresses," a Florida social worker told me.

Many foster parents join together to form their own support group. The Foster Parents Association in our county publishes a newsletter and sponsors special family events. Because they work together as a group, they have a strong voice in the local foster-care program.

For Further Reading:

Bell, Valerie. *Nobody's Children*. Dallas: Word Publishing, 1989.

Brown, Beth E. *When You're Mom No. 2*. Ann Arbor, Michigan: Servant Publications, 1991.

Cullen, Paul. *Stepfamilies, a Catholic Guide*. Huntington, Indiana: Our Sunday Visitor, Inc, 1989.

Houck, Don and LaDean. *Remarried with Children*. San Bernardino, California: Here's Life Publishers, 1991.

Hunt, Gary and Angela. *Mom and Dad Don't Live Together Anymore*. San Bernardino, California: Here's Life Publishers, 1989.

Johnson, Carolyn. *How to Blend a Family*. Grand Rapids, Michigan: Zondervan Publishing House, 1989.

Payne, C.J. *Caring for Deprived Children*. New York: St. Martin's Press, 1979.

Prilik, Pearl Ketover. *Stepmothering*. Los Angeles: Forman Publishers, 1988.

Rosin, Mark Bruce. *Stepfathering*. New York: Ballantine Books, 1987.

Rowe, Janet. *Long Term Foster Care*. New York: St Martin's Press, 1984.

White, Spike and Darnell. *I Need You! Being Friends with Your Grandkids*. Sisters, Oregon: Questar Publishers, 1989.

ENDNOTES

Chapter 1. The Step-in Parent

1. Clifton Fadiman, ed., *The Little, Brown Book of Anecdotes* (Boston: Little, Brown and Company, 1985), p. 328.
2. Fadiman, *The Little, Brown Book,* p. 60.

Chapter 2. Why Love Someone Else's Child?

1. G. Thomas, "Experts Sound Alarm about Rise in Crimes Committed by Kids," *Rocky Mountain News,* January 3, 1987, p. 8.
2. Glen Hester, quoted in Dr. Ken Magid and Carole McKelvey's *High Risk: Children Without a Conscience* (New York: Bantam Books, 1987), p. 155.
3. Marcia Slacum Greene, "The Crack Legacy: Children in Distress," *Washington Post,* September 10, 1989, p. a01.
4. Betty Webb, "Doubling the Danger of Divorce," *St. Petersburg Times,* January 9, 1991, p. 1D.
5. Paul Glick, "American Families: As They Are and Were," quoted in *The Family in America,* September 1990, p. 1.
6. Mark Bruce Rosin, *Stepfathering* (New York: Ballantine Books, 1987), p. 12.
7. Kim Painter, "Stepfamily Ties Are Binding More Children," *USA Today,* September 1, 1989, p. 01D.
8. Diane Mason, "Married to the Mob," *St. Petersburg Times,* September 3, 1988, p. 1D.
9. Valerie Bell, *Nobody's Children* (Dallas: Word Publishing, 1989), pp. 19–20.
10. Nancy Gibbs, "How America Has Run Out of Time," *Time,* April 24, 1989, p. 58.
11. Donna L. Hall, "Institutions of Marriage and Family to Survive," *Lynchburg News and Daily Advance,* 1981.
12. Gibbs, "America," pp. 63–64.
13. Tom Seligson, "Wanted: A Permanent Home," *Parade Magazine,* July 31, 1988, p. 4.
14. Magid and McKelvey, *High Risk,* p. 65.
15. Kitty Dumas, "Training the Grandparents to Take Care of Children," *Philadelphia Inquirer,* January 8, 1989, p. N14.
16. Nicholas Zill and Charlotte A. Schoenborn, "Developmental, Learning and Emotional Problems: Health of Our

Nation's Children, United States, 1988," quoted in *The Family in America*, March 1991, pp. 1–2.

17. "Kids Who Kill," *Good Housekeeping*, August 1989, p. 54.
18. "When 'Families' Will Have a New Definition," *U.S. News and World Report*, May 9, 1983, quoted in *Focus on the Family Newsletter*, July 1987.
19. Arthur J. Norton, "Families and Children in the Year 2000," *Children Today*, July–August 1987, p. 7.
20. Edith Schaeffer, *What is a Family?* (Old Tappan, New Jersey: Fleming H. Revell, 1975), pp. 121, 132, 147.

Chapter 3. Who Loves Other People's Children?

1. Barbara Kantrowitz and Pat Wingert, "Step by Step," *Newsweek Special Issue: The 21st Century Family*, August 1988, p. 25.
2. My husband and I wrote *Mom and Dad Don't Live Together Anymore* specifically for children who are dealing with the pain of divorce. It is geared for ages 9–15 and is available through Here's Life Publishers.
3. Kantrowitz and Wingert, "Step," p. 24.
4. John Patton and Brian Childs, "What Should We Call Them Now?" *Christian Family*, August 1988, p. 25.
5. Mark Bruce Rosin, *Stepfathering* (New York: Ballantine Books, 1987), p. 20.
6. Rosin, *Stepfathering*, p. 55.
7. Joan Libman, "Remarriages Are Creating Complex Families with Problems 'The Brady Bunch' Never Faced," *Los Angeles Times*, January 5, 1990, View.
8. Emily and John Visher, *How to Win as a Stepfamily* (New York: Dembner Books, 1982), p. 151.
9. Jill Smolowe, "To Grandma's House We Go," *Time*, November 5, 1990, p. 86.
10. David Larsen, "At an Age They Least Expect It, More Grandparents Are Rearing Young Children," *Los Angeles Times*, May 22, 1988, pp. 1–6.
11. James F. Kennedy, "Group Psychotherapy with Grandparents Rearing Their Emotionally Disturbed Grandchildren," *University of Louisville School of Medicine, Child Psychiatric Services*, 1987 Spring Volume, pp. 15–25.
12. Edith Fine, "Second Time Around for Grandparents Often Can Be Trying," *Los Angeles Times*, February 8, 1987, View, p. 1.

13. Sheryl McCarthy, "Raising Kids in 'Kinship'," *Newsday*, November 14, 1990, p. 06.
14. David Larsen, "Becoming a Parent Again," *Los Angeles Times*, May 22, 1988, View, p. 1.
15. Spike and Darnell White, *I Need You* (Sisters, Oregon: Questar Publishing, 1988), p. 175.
16. Fine, "Second Time Around," View, p. 1.
17. Mary Ann Kuharski, "Adoption from the Inside," *New Covenant*, June 1990, p. 12.
18. The story of Nick and Joan Granitsas is told in Susan Solomon Yem's article, "This House is Always Open," *Christian Parenting Today*, January/February 1991, pp. 29–31.
19. Jessica Siegel, "Church Families Open Up Homes, Hearts to Teens," *Chicago Tribune*, May 6, 1988, p. C7.
20. Mary Cronin, Melissa Ludtke, and James Willwerth, "Innocent Victims," *Time*, May 13, 1991, p. 57.
21. "Godparents: Love and Responsibility," *USA Today*, May 1988, p. 10.
22. David Diamond, "Filling the Grandparent Gap," *50 Plus*, May 1988, p. 42.
23. Jeanne E. Griffith, Mary J. Frase, and John H. Ralph, "American Education: The Challenge of Change," quoted in *The Family in America*, July 1990, p. 4.

Chapter 4. Taking the First Step

1. Adapted from Valerie Bell, *Nobody's Children* (Dallas: Word Publishing, 1989), pp. 95–98.
2. Nick Stinnett and John DeFrain, "Six Secrets of Strong Families," *Reader's Digest*, November 1987, p. 132.
3. Phyllis Coons, "Workshop Helps Stepfamilies Adjust to Losses and Gains," *Boston Globe*, December 26, 1980, Living, p. 1.
4. Adapted from Pearl Ketover Prilik, *Stepmothering: Another Kind of Love* (Los Angeles: Forman Publishing, 1988), pp. 22–26.
5. Prilik, *Stepmothering*, pp. xiii, xv.
6. Jon Nordheimer, "Dad as Pinch Hitter," *St. Petersburg Times*, October 22, 1990, p. 1D.
7. Prilik, *Stepmothering*, p. 15.
8. Prilik, *Stepmothering*, p. 56.
9. Adapted from Kathy Bence's "Attitudes and Acceptance," *Christian Family*, August 1988, p. 24.

Chapter 5. Adjustments, Big and Small

1. Mark Bruce Rosin, *Stepfathering* (New York: Ballantine Books, 1987), p. 79.
2. Amanda Morgan, "Happy Stepfamilies: What Are They Doing Right?" *Redbook*, May 1989, p. 129.
3. Morgan, "Happy Stepfamilies," p. 170.
4. Dolores Curran, "What Is a Healthy Family?" *Redbook*, June 1985, p. 89.
5. Curran, "Healthy Family," p. 89.
6. Emily Visher, quoted in Morgan, "Happy Stepfamilies," p. 170.
7. Claire Berman, "Stepparenting: How to Make It Work," *McCall's*, November 1989, pp. 97–99.
8. Michele Ingrassia, "Love and Remarriage the Second Time Around," *Newsday*, March 11, 1991, Part II, p. 42.
9. Eileen Ogintz, "To Stepfamilies, Holidays Mean Crossing the Great Divide," *Chicago Tribune*, December 18, 1988, p. 1C.
10. Ogintz, "Holidays," p. 1C.
11. Susan Duff and Dr. Amy Glaser, "Family Clinic," *Newsday*, November 19, 1988, Part II, p. 05.
12. Penelope Moffet, "Stepfamilies and Holidays: The Ties that Often Tangle," *Los Angeles Times*, December 23, 1986, pt. 5, p. 1.
13. Dr. Lee Salk, "Christmas under the New Family Tree," *Harper's Bazaar*, December 1987, p. 126.
14. Quoted in Alison Bass, "Stepparents Must Tread Lightly," *Boston Globe*, December 10, 1990, Health and Science, p. 10.
15. Salk, "Christmas," p. 126.
16. Marguerite Kelly, "Of Love and Money," *Washington Post*, October 22, 1987, p. e05.

Chapter 6. Defining Roles

1. Pearl Ketover Prilik, *Stepmothering: Another Kind of Love* (Los Angeles: Forman Publishing, 1988), p. 21.
2. Maria Krysan, Kristin A. Moore, and Nicholas Zill, "Research on Families," quoted in *The Family in America*, November 1990, p. 4.
3. Janice Mall, "USC Study Ponders Stepmother's Plight," *Los Angeles Times*, September 14, 1986, pt.6, p. 17.
4. Prilik, *Stepmothering*, p. 39.

5. Sally Squires, "White House to Main Street," *Washington Post*, November 24, 1987, p. z12.
6. Angela E. Hunt, "Learning to Speak the Same Language," *Sunday Digest*, June–August 1991, pp. 4–5.
7. Sandra Arbetter, "The Way It Is: The Remarried Family," *Current Health 2*, March 1989, p. 18.
8. Joshua Fischman, "The Trouble with Stepfathers," *Chicago Tribune*, December 31, 1989, p. 1C.
9. Jon Nordheimer, "Dad as Pinch Hitter," *St. Petersburg Times*, October 22, 1990, p. 2D.
10. Dorothy Sangster, "Making Stepparenting Work," *Chatelaine*, April 1990, p. 124.
11. Nordheimer, "Pinch Hitter," p. 2D.
12. Dr. Martin Goldberg, quoted in Bibi Wein, "The Special Stresses of Second Marriages," *Redbook*, June 1987, p. 152.
13. Mark Bruce Rosin, "How to Be Fair All Around," *WD's New Family*, June 28, 1988, p. 135.
14. Rosin, "Fair," p. 135.
15. Rosin, "Fair," p. 144.
16. Fischman, "Trouble," p. 1C.
17. Prilik, *Stepmothering*, p. 220.

Chapter 7. The Others Who Influence Your Family

1. Mark Bruce Rosin, *Stepfathering* (New York: Ballantine Books, 1987), p. 23.
2. John and Emily Visher, *How to Win as a Stepfamily* (New York: Dembner Books, 1982), pp. 94–95.
3. Visher and Visher, *How to Win*, p. 100.
4. Randy Greene, "Yours, Mine, and Ours: Can Stepfamilies Ever Blend?" *US Catholic*, July 1987, p. 35.
5. Rosin, *Stepfathering*, p. 63.
6. Rosin, *Stepfathering*, p. 64.
7. "Here's to Fathers Who Stepped In," *St. Petersburg Times*, June 16, 1991.
8. Frank F. Furstenberg, Jr., and Kathleen M. Harris, "The Disappearing American Father? Divorce and the Waning Significance of Biological Parenthood," quoted in *The Family in America*, October 1990, p. 2.
9. Andrew J. Cherlin and Frank F. Furstenberg, Jr., *The New American Grandparent* (New York: Basic Books, 1986), pp. 4–5.
10. Cherlin and Furstenberg, *Grandparent*, p. 50.

11. Janet Finch and Jennifer Mason, "Divorce, Remarriage, and Family Obligations," quoted in *The Family in America,* December 1990, p. 2.
12. Cherlin and Furstenberg, *Grandparent,* p. 156.
13. Cherlin and Furstenberg, *Grandparent,* p. 161.
14. Visher and Visher, *How to Win,* pp. 125–29.
15. Pamela Redmond Satran, "Parents and Grandparents at Odds," *Woman's Day,* June 16, 1987, p. 74.
16. Bibi Wein, "The Special Stresses of Second Marriages," *Redbook,* June 1987, p. 154.
17. Wein, "Special Stresses," p. 154.
18. *Bartlett's Familiar Quotations* (Boston: Little, Brown and Company, 1980), p. 914.

Chapter 8. Understanding a Child's Sense of Loss and Loyalty

1. Sally Squires, "White House to Main Street; Stepfamilies," *Washington Post,* November 24, 1987, Health, p. z12.
2. Emily and John Visher, *How to Win as a Stepfamily* (New York: Dembner Books, 1982), p. 16.
3. Squires, "White House," p. z12.
4. Lesley Dormen, "When You Like Your Stepparent Too Much," *Seventeen,* October 1987, pp. 152–53.
5. Squires, "White House," p. z12.
6. Quoted in Dormen, "When You Like," p. 153.
7. Edith H. Fine and Judith P. Josephson, "Second Time Around for Grandparents Often Can Be Trying," *Los Angeles Times,* February 8, 1987, View, p. 1.
8. Claire Berman, "Stepparenting: How to Make It Work," *McCall's,* November 1989, p. 100.
9. Berman, "Stepparenting," p. 101.
10. Dolores Curran, "What Is a Healthy Family?" *Redbook,* June 1985, p. 164.
11. Susan Perry, "Learning a Parenting Role, Step by Step," *Los Angeles Times,* August 13, 1987, View, p. 22.
12. Joan Libman, "If It's Saturday, This Must Be Daddy's House," *Working Mother,* December 1989, p. 66.
13. Libman, "Saturday," p. 68.

Chapter 9. Your Responsibilities and Rights

1. Joan Libman, "Remarriages Are Creating Complex

Families with Problems 'The Brady Bunch' Never Faced," *Los Angeles Times,* January 5, 1990, View, p. 1.

2. Mark Bruce Rosin, *Stepfathering* (New York: Ballantine Books, 1987), p. 51.
3. Michele Ingrassia, "Love and Remarriage: His, Hers, and Ours," *Newsday,* March 14, 1991, Part II, p. 68.
4. Ingrassia, "His, Hers, and Ours," p. 68.
5. Libman, "Remarriages," p. 1.
6. Jay Kesler, quoted in *Family Happiness Is Homemade,* May 1991, p. 1.
7. Emily and John Visher, *How to Win as a Stepfamily* (New York: Dembner Books, 1982), p. 65.
8. Anne Lorimer and Dr. Philip Feldman, "Getting Through the Trying Times That Every Stepfamily Must Face," *Philadelphia Inquirer,* January 27, 1985, p. K05.
9. Paul Cullen, *Stepfamilies: A Catholic Guide* (Huntington, Indiana: Our Sunday Visitor Publishing Division, 1988), p. 110.
10. Rosin, *Stepfathering,* p. 87.
11. Cullen, *Catholic Guide,* p. 118.
12. Ronaleen R. Roha, "Stepparents Have Rights, but Not Many," *Changing Times,* April 1987, p. 66.
13. "Stepparents Need Legal Clout," *McCall's,* May 1990, p. 66.
14. Edith H. Fine and Judith P. Josephson, "Second Time Around for Grandparents Often Can Be Trying," *Los Angeles Times,* February 8, 1987, View, p. 1.
15. Fine and Josephson, "Second Time Around," p. 1.
16. "Stepparents Need Legal Clout," p. 66.
17. Richard S. Victor, "Grandparent and Stepparent Rights: Assuring Visitation to the Child's Extended Family," *Trial,* April 1989, p. 59.
18. Ross A. Thompson, "Grandparents' Visitation Rights: Legalizing the Ties that Bind," *American Psychologist* 44 (1989): 1220.
19. Roha, "Stepparents Have Rights," p. 66.
20. Roha, "Stepparents Have Rights," p. 63.
21. Barbara Kantrowitz, "Children Lost in the Quagmire," *Newsweek,* May 13, 1991, p. 64.
22. Kantrowitz, "Quagmire," p. 64.

Chapter 10. When Changes Come

1. Susan Donim, "Confessions of a Wicked Stepmother," *Boston Globe,* May 25, 1980.

2. Ann Patchett, "Step-Siblings," *Seventeen,* June 1991, pp. 64–65.
3. Janet L. Bailey, "Letter to Carolyn," *Family Forum,* June 1991, p. 8.
4. Paul Lewis, "Long Distance Dads," *Focus on the Family,* September 1989, p. 8.
5. Catherine Phillips, "A Stepfamily's Dilemma," *Chatelaine,* July 1987, p. 26.
6. Phillips, "Dilemma," p. 26.
7. Sally Squires, "White House to Main Street: Stepfamilies," *Washington Post,* November 24, 1987, p. z12.
8. Paul Cullen, *Stepfamilies: A Catholic Guide* (Huntington, Indiana: Our Sunday Visitor Publishing Division, 1988), p. 116.

Chapter 11. Too Angry for Words

1. "Coping: A Primer for Stepparents," *Washington Post,* April 4, 1989, p. e05.
2. Stacey Burling, "Seminar Teaches the Path toward Stepfamily Bliss," *Philadelphia Inquirer,* September 21, 1989, p. c24.
3. "Coping," p. e05.
4. Michael Vitez, "Caution, Stepparents," *Philadelphia Inquirer,* December 26, 1991, p. E01.
5. "Coping," p. e05.
6. Anne Lorimer and Dr. Philip Feldman, "Getting Through the Trying Times That Every Stepfamily Must Face," *Philadelphia Inquirer,* January 27, 1985, p. K05.
7. Michele Ingrassia, "Love and Remarriage: The Battle of the Exes," *Newsday,* March 12, 1991, Part II, p. 39.
8. Ingrassia, "Battle," p. 39.
9. Ingrassia, "Battle," p. 39.
10. Claire Berman, "Stepparenting: How to Make It Work," *McCall's,* November 1989, p. 100.
11. Quoted in Berman, "Stepparenting," p. 100.
12. Ingrassia, "Battle," p. 39.
13. Ingrassia, "Battle," p. 39.
14. Pearl Ketover Prilik, *Stepparenting: Another Kind of Love* (Los Angeles: Forman Publishing, 1988), p. 95.
15. Lorimer and Feldman, "Getting Through," p. K05.
16. Ingrassia, "Battle," p. 39.
17. Robert W. Sweet, Jr., "Missing Children: Found Facts," quoted in *The Family in America,* May 1991, p. 1.

18. Beverly Raphael, "The Impact of Parental Loss on Adolescents' Psychological Characteristics," quoted in *The Family in America,* May 1991, p. 4.
19. Joshua Fischman, "The Trouble with Stepfathers: For Many Stepdaughters, 'Cinderella' Got It All Wrong," *Chicago Tribune,* December 31, 1989, p. 1C.
20. Buddy Scott, *Relief for Hurting Parents* (Nashville: Oliver Nelson Books, 1989), p. 10.
21. Personal interview with Buddy Scott, February 6, 1990.
22. The women's stories are told by David Larsen, "Becoming a Parent Again," *Los Angeles Times,* May 22, 1988, View, p. 1.
23. James Kennedy, "Group Psychotherapy with Grandparents Rearing Their Emotionally Disturbed Grandchildren," *University of Louisville School of Medicine, Child Psychiatric Services,* 1987 Spring Volume 11(1) pp. 15–25.
24. James Kennedy, "The Extended Family Revisited: Grandparents Rearing Grandchildren," *Child Psychiatry and Human Development,* 1988 Fall Volume 19(1) pp. 26–35.
25. Paul Cullen, *Stepfamilies: A Catholic Guide* (Huntington, Indiana: Our Sunday Visitor Publishing Division, 1988), p. 51.
26. S. I. McMillen, M.D., *None of These Diseases* (Old Tappan, New Jersey: Fleming H. Revell Company, 1984), p. 116.
27. Karen S. Peterson, "Dealing with Anger and Guilt," *USA Today,* October 8, 1990, p. 2D.

Chapter 12. The Rewards of Loving Someone Else's Child

1. David Kopp, "Dreaming of Home," *Christian Parenting Today,* March/April 1991, p. 8.
2. Quoted by Randy Greene, "Yours, Mine, and Ours: Can Stepfamilies Ever Blend?" *U.S. Catholic,* July 1987, p. 32.
3. Greene, "Blend," p. 37.
4. Betty Rex, as told to Barbara Pierce, "The Tears—and Rage—of a Foster Mother," *Redbook,* July 1987, p. 37.
5. Joshua Fischman, "The Trouble with Stepfathers: For Many Stepdaughters, 'Cinderella' Got It All Wrong," *Chicago Tribune,* December 31, 1989, p. 1C.
6. Joshua Fischman, "Trouble."
7. Nick Stinnett and John DeFrain, "Six Secrets of Strong Families," *Reader's Digest,* November 1987, p. 135.

8. Zill, Furstenberg, and Bray are quoted in Sally Squires, "White House to Main Street; Stepfamilies," *Washington Post,* November 24, 1987, p. z12.
9. Emily and John Visher, *How to Win as a Stepfamily* (New York: Dembner Books, 1982) p. 151.
10. Lynda Barry, "Guardian Neighbor," *Newsweek* Special Issue, Summer 1991, pp. 70, 73.

A child you know between the ages of 10-14 may enjoy these stories about Cassie Perkins, a young teen adjusting to a stepfamily.

The Cassie Perkins series
also by Angela Elwell Hunt

#1 No More Broken Promises. Cassie surprises herself when she wins the lead in the school musical. But she loses confidence in her ability when her father moves out.

#2 A Forever Friend. Cassie wants to go to the School for the Performing Arts, but her parents are not enthusiastic about it. She finds an unlikely ally in her mother's boyfriend—whom she can't stand.

#3 A Basket of Roses. Cassie feels out of place in her new school, and life gets more complicated when her mother decides to remarry. Cassie vows to stop her mother's new romance.

#4 A Dream to Cherish. Back at her old school, Cassie doesn't seem to fit in until a popular senior befriends her! Now Cassie's life is going *her* way—until she gets some shocking news.

#5 The Much-Adored Sandy Shore. If it's the last thing she does, Cassie's going to prove she's not self-centered. And she's found the perfect person to help her—Sandy, the school outcast!

#6 Love Burning Bright. Cassie loves everything about summer camp—except Ethan Wilcox, the camp jerk. So why is Cassie so drawn to him?